THE AUTHORITY OF THE PAST

AAR STUDIES IN RELIGION
1970:1

THE AUTHORITY OF THE PAST

A Study of Three Muslim Modernists

by

SHEILA MCDONOUGH
Associate Professor of Religion
Sir George Williams University, Montreal

Chambersburg, Pennsylvania
American Academy of Religion
1970

Library of Congress Catalog Card Number: 76-141690

Copyright © American Academy of Religion

PRINTED IN THE UNITED STATES OF AMERICA

PRINTING DEPARTMENT, UNIVERSITY OF MONTANA, MISSOULA, MONTANA, 59801

Table of Contents

Introduction

Our purpose is to discuss the ideas of three Muslim modernists in relation to the question "What is the authority of the past?" The three are Sayyid Ahmad Khan (1817-1898), Muhammad Iqbal (1873-1938), and Ghulam Ahmad Parwez (1903-   ). These men represent instances of Muslim modernism as developed in India in the mid-nineteenth century, the early twentieth century, and in Pakistan since Independence. The first two are figures of major importance, whereas the third is minor. All three share much common vocabulary, and many assumptions. The differences between them reflect partly the changes in situation of the Muslim community in the periods under discussion, partly varieties in intellectual climate, and partly the personalities of the three. The last, Parwez, represents in some measure the state of mind of contemporary unhappy Pakistani young people—those who are products of a westernized education, yet hostile to the West, the communist world, and their own tradition. His work is interesting as a manifestation of one type of popular modernism.

It is evident that the effort to articulate how much authority, if any, the past should exercise over the present, and the emerging future must be a central concern of modernist thinking. Authority means here the felt legitimacy of patterns of life, social and ethical codes, as well as the articulated legitimization of these traditional ways of life. Since the Muslim way of life is founded on God's gracious act of revelation, a tension exists between what the life-styles might be at any time, as opposed to what the community believes they ought to be. Sometimes, the two may be indistinguishable, but it is equally possible for a wide disparity to exist. Usually, the "ought" is some degree in advance of "what is."

As long as it is agreed that the Muslim way of life has some degree of legitimacy, the assumption that ultimate authority rests with God is usually present. It is also possible to argue for the continuance of Muslim culture as an end in itself, and some modernists attempt something like this. Such a position is perhaps more possible in a traditional Muslim society where the land and political power are in Muslim hands. But with the collapse of the power of the Mughal Empire in India, neither control of land nor control over their own political development was necessarily going to remain with Muslims. Thus the modernists in this instance had to try to deal with the problems concomitant with industrialization, the scientific revolution, and rapid social change along with the additional difficulty of loss of control of India. The crisis precipitated by the loss of Muslim power may have added a special dimension of urgency to Indian Muslim feeling that God had abandoned them. It seems to be true that debate as to what God is doing, intends to do and will do, seems to have taken

1

place with more vigor, and more diversity of opinion among these Muslims than among any comparable group of their co-religionists.

Our method will be to give a summary of the fundamental ideas of each of the three, as well as a brief discussion of the different political and social contexts in which they lived and worked. Their respective lives, Sayyid Ahmad Khan (1817-1898), Muhammad Iqbal (1867-1938) and Ghulam Ahmad Parwez (1903-   ) overlap just to this extent: that each was coming to maturity as the previous one died. None of them received a classical theological education in the Muslim equivalent of a theological seminary, although Sayyid Ahmad Khan and Iqbal had a good knowledge of the Islamic tradition. We will refer to them as laymen in order to distinguish them from the *ulema*, those religious scholars who had received the traditional form of education. In Islam, the distinction between layman and religious scholar has no connotation other than that of educational background, since the institution of a priesthood with a sacramental function does not exist in a form comparable to ordained priesthood in the West. In Iqbal's case, the distinction between himself and the traditionalists is very like that which would exist in the West between someone who had studied a religious tradition in a university setting, and someone who had attended a conservative seminary.

Each of the three has written much on religious questions. Sayyid Ahmad Khan and Parwez have written lengthy commentaries on the Qur'an, and, although Iqbal did not explicitly do so, implicitly his writing is an attempt to articulate an understanding of the relevance of the Qur'an for his time. In referring to these three as modernists, we are attempting to present them as they have been regarded in their own community. Each of them is known to have undertaken to write his own views on religion, and to persuade the community to agreement. Thus it is well known that they have been infringing on the traditional role of the religious scholars, and the latter have not hesitated to object with vehemence. The label "modernist" is given by the products of the traditional training to all those who attempt, without the benefit of such training, to put forward their views.

The contrast between these three modernist religious authors and the traditional religious scholars, the *ulema*, is that the former received their education, religious and otherwise, elsewhere than in the organized religious schools (*madrasas*), and became authors, i.e. functioned primarily in the literate part of the society, while the latter were educated in, and kept a loose connection with, the institutionalized religious schools, and have been mainly active in their society by delivering the Friday sermons in the mosques. The illiterate people are generally reached only by the *ulema*. Here is, of course, the source of their constant influence since a large proportion of the population has always been and still is illiterate.

It is theoretically possible that a *madrasa*-educated man might have modernist, or innovative, opinions. Quite probably, this will happen more and more. There are noteworthy instances in other Muslim countries. But we want to stress the educational factor in the examples we are discussing, since it did mean that these three particular modernists, unlike many of their predecessors, acknowledged no institutionalized authority that could combat their views.

Although heresy and excommunication in precisely the Christian sense do not exist in Islam, the *ulema* have always had the option of condemning an idea as a dangerous innovation. The extent to which their judgment influences Muslim opinion generally has been directly related to the prestige of the institution of the religious scholars during the historical period in question. From the tenth century to the nineteenth, the authority of the instituion of the religious scholars was not seriously questioned. Thus relatively few innovations took place throughout that period. In the earlier phase of Islamic history, the seventh to the tenth centuries, the institution of religious scholars had not yet become formalized as it did in the later medieval times. One aspect of the contestation between our three modernists and the *ulema* is thus that the normative period for the latter is the medieval, whereas the former want to go back to the pre-medieval to find norms with which to challenge the beliefs and practices of the present. In the pre-medieval phase, everyone could be considered to have been a layman, and that includes all those who were companions of the Prophet, those who developed the laws and the theology of early Islam, and those who worked out devices which enabled the community to conquer and to survive. Education in a *madrasa* does not encourage students to envisage Islamic history in this way as the work of laymen, but university training is more likely to encourage such a perspective.

Given that "modernist" in our context implies one who has theological opinions without having had traditional training, it follows that a diversity of theories can be expected from such "free-thinking" minds. Even using only three instances, we will discover radically different views on fundamental issues such as the validity of personal religious experience, and the transcendence or immanence of God. Such fragmentation of opinion would seem to be an inexorable consequence of abandoning any institutionalized way of debating the validity of new ideas and interpretations of traditional values. Yet each of these three men is trying to persuade the community to accept his views. Their path has been an individual one, but none takes the view that religion is an individual and private matter. They are none of them advocating a situation in which every Muslim can believe as he likes. The reason for this concern is that each of these modernists is motivated by anxiety about the future of the community. Each thinks that misguided religious beliefs and practices are causes of the general backwardness of the Muslim people. Therefore each puts forward his novel religious ideas in the expectation that religious change is a necessary instrument for change in the people's general situation. From such a conviction, the modernists in question conclude that something is fundamentally wrong with beliefs and practices that could have such derogatory effects. This position leads them to think of the traditional religious leaders as adversaries of essential change, and as inadequate exponents of the faith.

Sayyid Ahmad Khan

THE Muslim presence in India had begun with the Arab invasion of Sind in 711. In the following centuries various Muslim armies came into the North-West. There were also Muslim traders operating in some other parts of India. The Mughal Empire was founded by Babur (1483-1530), a Turk from Central Asia who claimed descent from Timur on his father's side and from Chengis Khan on his mother's side. His grandson, Akbar (1542-1606), ruled brilliantly for fifty years. At his death, the Mughal Empire controlled about two-thirds of the territory that now is divided into the two nations of India and Pakistan.[1]

The British presence in India increased steadily in the late seventeenth and eighteenth centuries as a result of the vigorous efforts of the East India Company. By the mid-nineteenth century, the East India Company had virtual control of most of the sub-continent. But the Mughal Emperor and his court were still present in Delhi in the first part of the century, and continued to exercise nominal authority. In 1857 the event known at the time as "The Mutiny" occurred. Indian troops serving in the British army rebelled against their British officers, and violence spread quickly. Many Europeans were killed before the British finally suppressed the Revolt.

The occasion of the Revolt is said to have been the use of greased cartridges, although most historians now think that incident was just a spark that set off a situation full of explosive tensions. The British were furious at the massacres of their people. They were particularly harsh in reprisals against the Mughal court, since they seem to have feared that the main threat to their position probably lay with the Muslims. The last Mughal Emperor died, and his palace was razed to the ground.

The first of the Muslim modernists under discussion, Sayyid Ahmad Khan, was forty at the time of the Indian Revolt of 1857. He had been a sub-judge. As one commentator puts it:

"Himself, a relic of the palmy days of the Great Mughals, he ushered in a new era. He gave the Indian Muslims a new prose, a new approach to the individual and national problems, and built up an organization which could carry on his work. Before this there was all disintegration and decay. He rallied together the Indian Muslims, and became the first prophet of their new nationhood."[2]

---

[1] An excellent and very readable source for information about Muslims in India is P. Spear, *A History of India*, Harmondsworth, Penguin Books, 1965.

[2] From Abdul Qayyum, "Jinnah and Islam," in *The Cultural Heritage of Pakistan*, eds. S. M. Ikram and P. Spear, Karachi, Oxford University Press, 1955, p. 188.

The phrase "himself, a relic" is the key to Sayyid Ahmad Khan's situation. He had received his education in the very sheltered home of Muslim aristocrats in Mughal Delhi. His biographer, Hali, has shown us the family background of the great reformer in the last days of the Mughal court in Delhi. The young aristocrat grew up in an atmosphere of serenity; he lived almost entirely within the limits of his family's property, and played with his own relatives. His mother was distinguished by the independence of her mind, and by her freedom from the superstitions common to many Indian women. Through his relatives, Sayyid Ahmad Khan was in contact with much of the intellectual and spiritual life of the leaders of the Muslim community. He saw the dignity of his people while they were still their own masters.[3]

The decisive event that transformed him from an ordinary civil servant into an impassioned reformer was the Mutiny of 1857. One can perhaps see the key to the shape of Sayyid Ahmad Khan's modernism in his reaction to this shattering experience. Overnight the world of the Mughal court, the basis of the serene world of his childhood, disappeared. The bubble of the illusion of Muslim power was pricked, and the community was left, for the first time in history, a subject people. Moreover, it looked as though the British might be prepared to inflict much more humiliation and disgrace on the Muslims. The Revolt precipitated him personally into what might well be characterized as an extreme "boundary situation," since he had lived after the death of his world. If one is a relic, there is a strong pressure to recede into dimness.

A Muslim writer described Sayyid Ahmad Khan's experiences as follows:

"Events of 1857-58 constituted a great national tragedy, but to judge by all appearances, Sayyid Ahmad himself had not fared badly. He emerged out of the conflict without doing anything which could cause him remorse, either as a loyal Government servant or as a patriotic Indian. The Revolt had also provided him with an opportunity to write a book, which at once brought him into the front rank of the leaders of Indian opinion. Apparently, Sayyid Ahmad himself had not been affected adversely by the course of events, but if we study his speeches and writings of this period, we feel that this was the greatest blow he ever suffered. His sorrow and anguish was unlimited. The grief turned his hair prematurely grey, and completely changed the course of his life.

"The reasons for this intense and sharp reaction were twofold—both personal and national. Sayyid Ahmad himself was unhurt, but his near and dear ones had suffered terribly during the reprisals which the British encouraged or countenanced after the fall of Delhi. His mother was at the Mughal capital during the disturbances, and when he went to visit her after the British occupation of the city, this heart-breaking sight met his eyes:

"On reaching his house, he heard that his mother had taken refuge in one of her syce's (horse-attendant's) houses and he followed her there. On his calling out to her, she opened the door, crying: 'Why have you come here? All are

[3] Altaf Husayn Hali, *Hayat-i Jaivid*, Lahore, Nur Company, 1957, pp. 77-104.

being killed. You will be killed also.' He told her not to be afraid, as he had a special pass. He then found out that for five days she had been living on the horses' grain and was very weak. For three days she had had no water. He took his mother back with him to Meerut, but what she had undergone was too much for her and in spite of the best medical assistance she died within a month. 'Sayyid Ahmad's uncle and cousin, whose house adjoined his at Delhi, were slain unarmed by the infuriated Sikhs three days after the assault.' Graham, who has recorded all this, adds: 'They were as loyal as Sayyid Ahmad himself, but at that dreadful time many innocent men, I grieve to say, suffered for the sins of the guilty.'[4]

"Sayyid Ahmad's personal loss was heavy, but when he saw what the Muslim community had suffered, his grief was inconsolable. In the indiscriminate massacre, arson and loot which followed the British occupation of the city, Delhi, which Sayyid Ahmad had known so well and loved so tenderly, simply ceased to exist. The British quarrel was really with the mutineers and their comrades in arms. But partly to strike terror in the minds of Indians in general, and partly out of anger at the mad massacre of European women and children at the hands of the mutineers, the authorities unleashed the dogs of war on the vast civil population of the city. Besides, in order to enlist the support of the Sikh soldiery, the Punjab officials had by narrating legendary tales stirred their religious zeal to the white heat of fanaticism and, in this hypnotised state, the Sikh soldiers committed atrocities which were more revolting than even those committed by the angry British soldiers. What Delhi suffered in these conditions is hard to describe, but easy to imagine. Not a house was safe; not a human being was secure. For several days after the British occupation of Delhi, civilians were shot at sight and when this was over, trials under the Martial Law started and any wretch who had a grievance against another or who wanted to win the favor of the victors, would come forward with accusation of complicity against the best and the noblest, and was readily believed. All the celebrities of Delhi, whom Sayyid Ahmad had described in his *Asar-ul-Sanadid*, were dead or were hiding to save their lives. The vast quarter of the city between the Fort and the grand mosque, which housed the Mughal aristocracy, was completely razed to the ground and ploughed up. The grand mosque of Shah Jahan was taken over by the army, and the Anglo-Indian press was freely debating whether it should be destroyed or converted into a church!

"Sayyid Ahmad's grief at what he saw was boundless. He felt that India was no place for a self-respecting Muslim and wanted to retire from service and settle in Egypt. About this time, Shakespeare, whose life he had saved at Bijnore, wanted to recommend him for the grant of the taluka [estate] of

---

[4] Quoted from G. F. I. Graham, *Life of Sayed Ahmed Khan*, Edinburgh, Blackwood, 1885, p. 12.

Chandpur. Sayyid Ahmad, however, refused to be enriched by the grant of a taluka, which had been forfeited as punishment to a Muslim talukdar, and informed Shakespeare that he did not want to stay in India. He later stated in a public speech, recalling those fearful days:

"'At that time I did not believe that my people would regain even something of their prosperity, and I could not bear to see the condition, in which they were at that time. . . . Believe me, this grief aged me and my hair turned grey.'

"Luckily Sayyid Ahmad did not yield to the counsel of despair, and, realising that 'it would be an act of cowardice and selfishness to seek a haven of peace when one's people were in a desperate condition,' he gave up the idea of migration from India and chose the stony path of a hard struggle and patient, assiduous labor.

"He pondered over the tragedy which had overtaken his country and came to the conclusion that it was caused by ignorance. He, therefore, set himself to the task of educating both the ruler and the ruled, and removing the causes of possible friction and misunderstanding. The first task he had commenced with his *Causes of the Indian Revolt*, and he continued it throughout his life by a courageous representation of the viewpoint of his countrymen."[5]

How shall we explain or account for the vigor of his reaction? Although other Muslims followed him, his leadership was highly individual; he worked steadily for the next forty-one years agitating, haranguing his community, campaigning for money, and starting many projects. He had initially felt so much despair that he had considered leaving India. His decision to stay and work for specific goals was conscious. Although he was not fluent in English, he was somehow able to relate himself to nineteenth-century Western political and intellectual values without feeling threatened or undermined in the reserves of his own self-understanding and faith.

Though the British often annoyed him, he seems never to have suffered any serious doubt about his own capacities as over against India's new rulers. This confidence is perhaps a tribute to the qualities of dignity and self-respect a Mughal aristocrat absorbed from his upbringing in the midst of his family. Apparently, it never seriously entered the mind of Sayyid Ahmad that the difficulties of his community were anything other than temporary and more or less incidental. The firmness of the community's strength was axiomatic. Such a high degree of fundamental confidence in the roots of culture made possible a spirit of great adaptibility in practice. Sayyid Ahmad was ready to advocate many apparently radical changes in belief and practice, because his inner priorities were clear. The first priority was the successful transcendence by the community of its immediate difficulties so that it might recover strength and wellbeing.

Is this a religious perspective? Although many of Sayyid Ahmad Khan's

⁵ S. M. Ikram, *Modern Muslim India and the Birth of Pakistan*, 2nd edition, Lahore, Sh. Muhammad Ashraf, 1965, pp. 30-33.

reforms might have been advocated by men who were not believers, he was clear that it was his faith in God that shaped his activities. One of his most noted and controversial statements was:

"If that religion is in conformity with human nature, or with Nature in general, then it is true. . . . I am fully confident that the guidance which He has given us is absolutely in conformity with our constitution and our nature and this is the only touchstone of its truth."[6]

"Fully confident" is the most apt description of his faith. From this confidence, he was ready to attempt to synthesize anything new that might be true with all that was already known to be true. Since truth was in conformity with nature, the exercise of intelligence should solve, or at least shed illumination on, all apparently troublesome matters.

"The natural" seems to have meant to Sayyid Ahmad Khan the self-evidently right. In ethical matters, this seems to mean basic principles of justice and respect for individuals; he apparently learned these principles early and never saw any reason to question them, or their "naturalness." Probably, the good man was for him the kind of person his mother would have said was a good man. This was not a goodness of adherence to external practices, but of spirit and intention.

Sayyid Ahmad Khan emphasized the natural as a touchstone because he thought that much of the backwardness of the Muslims, as compared to the British, was a result of a false supernaturalism. His campaign for the revival of the community thus led him to attack all those beliefs that he thought the cause of retrogressive attitudes. Specifically, he considered belief in miracles wrong and unnatural. In order to help the community revise its understanding of these matters, he wrote a commentary on the Qur'an, and a treatise on the principles of Qur'anic exegesis.[7] He attempted to offer rational explanations for all the apparent miracles narrated by the Qur'an. In the case of the splitting of the Red Sea, for instance, he said that Moses led the people across at a time when the water was at its ebb. He said that the Red Sea was not so deep in those days, and that there were islands in it. As for the command to Moses to strike the sea with his rod, he said the world *daraba* does not mean, in this instance, to strike. He said it meant to walk. Moses had been commanded to walk into the sea.[8]

One of his most radical innovations was his denial of the Virgin Birth of Jesus.[9] And yet he also wrote a commentary on the Bible, apparently for the

---

[6] B. A. Dar, *Religious Thought of Sayyid Ahmad Khan*, Lahore Institute of Islamic Culture, 1957, pp. 149-50.

[7] Sayyid Ahmad Khan, *Tafsiru-l-Qur'an* (6 vols.), Lahore, Matba-i Gulzar - i Muhammadi, 1891. Sir Sayyid Ahmad Khan, *Tahrir fi usul al tafsir*, Lahore, Nuvalkishor Steam, 1913. An unpublished English translation by D. M. Rahbar is in the library of the Institute of Islamic Studies, McGill University.

[8] Sayyid Ahmad Khan, *Tafsiru-l-Qur'an*, vol. 1, pp. 77-92.

[9] *Ibid.*, vol. 2, pp. 15-35.

purpose of attempting to create a greater degree of mutual respect among Muslims and Christians.[10] No Muslim since his time has made a comparable attempt at detailed exegesis of both scriptures. The amount of work done by Sayyid Ahmad Khan indicates that he was a tireless worker at the causes he believed to be urgent. With some assistance from friends, he was trying to discover all that could be known by "modern" men about religion. This quest led him into the paths of nineteenth-century Biblical criticism and philosophy of religion. His attitude to the spiritual worth of the Bible was more positive than the traditional Muslim view. In his words:

"Upon the whole, it may be inferred that the Pentateuch of our time is the copy of the edition which Ezra himself wrote. Under the dictates of our religion we Mohomedans consider the existing Pentateuch executed under Divine instruction by Ezra, to be identical with that of Moses, of equal authenticity, and entitled to equal reverence; for both of them were Prophets of God, and there is no distinction of any kind allowed by us Mohomedans between the Prophets, for they are all from the same source."[11]

He explained as follows what he thought to be the meaning of the Qur'an narratives about creation, and the Adam's banishment from the Garden of Eden: Adam, as presented in the Qur'an, is not an individual, but a symbol for the whole human race. The importance of the story of Adam is that it throws light on human nature. The angels are the forces of nature by which the universe is operated; they are the potentialities latent in things.

The devil (Shaytan) is also a force that operates in man. Sayyid Ahmad Khan did not believe that the devil exists apart from man; he is a symbol for the passionate, unruly side of human nature. The Qur'anic narratives in which angels are told to bow before Adam, and in which the devil refuses the command, are understood by Sayyid Ahmad Khan to mean that God gives power to man over the forces of nature. He says that the devil's refusal means that man has power over the unruly side of his nature, but that this passionate temper is difficult to control and that it is always threatening rebellion.

Man's existence in paradise means to Sayyid Ahmad Khan the animal stage of existence before self-consciousness emerged. With self-consciousness, he says, the demonic side of man's nature also emerged. He believes that the story of Adam's rebellion is meant to teach the reality of God-given freedom.[12]

For Sayyid Ahmad Khan, the salvation of man lies in the developing of his capacity to respond to his conscience. Man should, he believes, acquire practice in doing good, and in rejecting the impulses from the demonic side of his nature. In his view, virtue is to be acquired through the active cultivation of the power to do good and to suppress evil impulses.

---

[10] Sayyid Ahmad Khan, *The Mohammedan Commentary on the Holy Bible*, Aligarh, 1865.

[11] *Ibid.*, part 2, p. 15.

[12] B. A. Dar, *Religious Thought of Sayyid Ahmad Khan*, pp. 133-176.

Sayyid Ahmad Khan is notably in the Sufi tradition in his use of allegorical interpretations of Qur'anic stories, and in his emphasis on purification of the self as the main business of a religious man. The originality of his thought lies in his equating the Qur'anic stories with the truths about the origins of life discovered by science. His idea of purification is also rather more moral than mystical in the Sufi sense. This latter emphasis may come in part from the Wahhabi (puritan) strain in Sayyid Ahmad Khan, although certainly one could say it is a normal Muslim view of the growth of the soul in response to God.

Although, as indicated, Sayyid Ahmad Khan was opposed to what he deemed "unnatural" supernaturalism, he nevertheless thought of God as transcendent. If anything, his efforts to disparage miracles were grounded in a feeling that God was beyond or remote from the possibility of such intervention in human affairs. He thought there had been an exaggerated preoccupation with personal prayer in traditional Islamic practice. Since he was concerned to urge Muslims to stir themselves out of sleepy conformity with traditional, and now futile, modes of life, he was greatly concerned to induce in them an awareness of the need to become self-conscious individuals, thinking through all their actions, and taking upon themselves the burden of personal responsibility. In this context, he thought recourse to prayer for direct intervention from God wrong. He pointed out that infinite numbers of prayers had failed to change the world. Prayer, he said, should be understood as the concentrating of the mind on God so that out of the sense of the majesty and power of God a mood of patience and acceptance might be attained by man. Prayer should have the effect of enabling man to bear with patience his afflictions.

With respect to heaven and hell, he took the view that the Qur'anic verses were allegories intended to teach man that he will receive happiness or unhappiness after death according to what he deserves in the light of his behavior on earth. He said that the nature of life after death could not be understood in any greater detail than this. He did not question the ultimate reality of final judgment.[13]

Sayyid Ahmad Khan's mood was essentially sober optimism; he seemed to believe that man is good, and that he can be expected by hard work, and by the cultivation of his natural powers, to learn to order the world in a just and reasonable way. He believed that God has established a universe based on law, and that men with the "light of nature" in their hearts are able to discern and follow these laws.[14] He implied that patience, tolerance, hard work, and virtue can be expected to overcome most difficulties.

Such closeness as there is between man and God would be from Sayyid Ahmad Khan's perspective in the area of conscience. He maintained that man had a natural ability to distinguish between right and wrong. Therefore the Qur'an appeals, and gives further guidance to, man who is already, in some

[13] Sayyid Ahmad Khan, *Tafsiru-l-Qur'an*, vol. 1, pp. 39-48.
[14] *Ibid*, pp. 23,24.

measure, on the right path. Normal human life is good; and sensible, hard-working people ought to be able to resolve their difficulties.

As might be expected, an openness in principle to persons of other religious traditions follows from this position. One of the most daring of Sayyid Ahmad Khan's immediate responses to the disaster of 1857 was a decision on his part to write and tell the British where they had been at fault.

"When Sayyid Ahmad Khan wanted to send his treatise *The Causes of the Mutiny* to the Parliament and the Government of India, a good friend of his advised him: 'Burn all these copies and do not expose yourself to danger.' Then Sayyid Ahmad Khan replied: . . . 'If I suffer some harm for such a cause which is profitable for the Empire and its subjects both, I shall bear it.' "[15]

His thesis was that the British had erred in showing contempt for Indians, and for failing to deal with their subjects in a manner befitting gentlemen. It is said that the letter had some influence on Allen Octavian Hume, the English-man who later founded the Congress Party so that Indians might begin to work towards self-government.[16]

One of ironies of this process of inter-action is that Sayyid Ahmad Khan himself rejected the possibility of working with the Hindus in the Congress when the latter was founded. In order to understand this development, we have to remember that his first priority was the survival and revival of the Muslim community. Sayyid Ahmad Khan had come into conflict with Hindu opinion over matters of priorities for language in India. One aspect of his concern was to work for the survival of Urdu, rather than Hindi, as an important source of Indian culture.

Sayyid Ahmad Khan was not advocating a secular, pluralist society, although he was trying to urge Muslims to relate themselves constructively to Western-ers—to dine with them, to respect their religion, to learn their sciences, and so forth. These efforts to change Muslim attitudes from contemptuous non-contact to respectful co-existence were all based on the assumption that such changes would be in the interest of the success of the community under the new condi-tions. Such a commitment, of course, implies that anything seen as a threat to the unity of the community, such as the loss of the Urdu language, must be com-batted. The religious assumption is that the continuance of the community as a separate cultural unit is God's will; Sayyid Ahmad Khan was compelled to his many years of purposeful striving by the conviction that the weakness in the community resulted from various human errors, laziness and complacency in particular. Thus his faith was that clearer thinking and harder work must bring the community closer to God, and to renewed success in the world. The fruits of his reforms were intended to be an ultimately stronger and more effective Muslim community.

[15] J. M. S. Baljon, *The Reforms and Religious Ideas of Sir Sayyid Ahmad Khan*, Leiden, Brill, 1949, p. 10.
[16] S. M. Ikram, *Modern Muslim India and the Birth of Pakistan*, p. 29.

What does it mean to say his aim was not a secular, pluralist society? He was certainly not advocating a society in which the *ulema*, the religious scholars, as they existed in his lifetime, would exercise political control. His efforts to change Muslim thinking about miracles and prayer and similar issues made him a kind of arch-fiend in the eyes of many of the *ulema*. They counter-attacked regularly by accusing him of many forms of heresy. The *ulema* of present-day Pakistan still often refer to him as an instance of disruptive bad thinking.

Since Sayyid Ahmad Khan had known at first hand the normal patterns of life of the Mughal Empire, it was not unnatural for him to assume as a matter of course that the *ulema* would not exercise political control, for they had never done so in the past of the Mughal and other Muslim empires. The degree to which an individual Mughal emperor had paid any attention to the *ulema* varied greatly and depended in part on matters of personality. One could perhaps say that Sayyid Ahmad Khan was advocating a society in which lay Muslims would exercise authority. This was the traditional position with respect to political authority. What was radical and shocking to the *ulema* was Sayyid Ahmad Khan's readiness as a layman to offer opinion on matters of faith and religious law. Here, too, he could and did appeal to the precedent of the original Muslim community, but lay activity of this kind had not been practiced for centuries. As we have indicated, he was driven to undertake theological disputation because of his conviction that it was in these areas that changes must be made quickly if the community was to survive.

In addition to his assaults on supernaturalism, he was led by the logic of his undertaking to dispute the accepted attitudes to the religious law, Shari'ah; and the traditions, Hadith. The general view was that on independent thinking on matters of religious law, *ijtihad*, the doors had been closed in the tenth century after two or three centuries in which scholars had carefully scrutinized all possible aspects of Muslim life. The conviction that the Shari'ah is fixed and unalterable is therefore a belief that the original scholars did their work so well that no new problems could arise and that nothing new could be said that might be true, good, or useful. Similarly, the decisions as to the authenticity of Hadith were made by scholars of the same early period. To reopen the question meant to claim equal ability and authority for a nineteenth-century man as compared to a ninth-century man in the area of deciding what the original norms of the community had been, and how the authority of those norms was to be applied in present circumstances. In part, Sayyid Ahmad Khan's argument can be seen as a critique of a particular religious institution, i.e. he was denying any final authority to the *ulema*, past and present, as an elite having unquestioned authority to interpret norms for the community.

In his efforts to explain how the Muslim community had arrived at its post-1857 depressed condition, Sayyid Ahmad Khan said that Muslims had possessed the "true religion" from the beginning, but they had later lost the proper spirit and had been misled by various forms of foreign influence. In his words:

"Many old Jewish stories and many Roman Catholic ideas and beliefs, and some ideas of an old Christian sect that existed a long time in Arabia, and many practices of the Hindus are adopted by us Muslims . . . and this is the reason why non-Muslims by equating Islam with these things view Islam with contempt."[17]

Sayyid Ahmad Khan often undertook to refute Western scholars who wrote what he considered inadequate or disparaging studies of Muslims. He intended to help bolster up the community's self-respect by demanding that Western scholars treat Islamic subjects with accuracy and justice. His firmness on such issues is another dimension of his own self-confidence; his greatest life work was his insistence that his community must learn modern scientific methods. But the great respect he felt for the knowledge of the West did not stop him from immediately reacting against particular Western scholars when he was convinced that they were not doing justice to the subject he knew. Doubtless most peoples who have been the object of Western research have felt discouraged and depressed by the portrayal of themselves that is put forward; what is remarkable about Sayyid Ahmad Khan is the immediacy and vigor of his response.[18]

In order to re-open the process of decision-making about norms, Sayyid Ahmad Khan had to go back to the Qur'an as the original authority for the community's existence. He maintained that the miraculous nature of the Qur'an lay in the fact that it offered wisdom and guidance of a kind far beyond the capacities of a man coming out of the low level of civilization prevalent in pre-Islamic Arabia. In his words:

"The proof that the Qur'an comes from God does not lie only in its eloquence . . . A person from such a backward nation could not without the light God had given him have produced such wisdom and guidance as is found in the Qur'an."[19]

The importance of the Qur'an is thus that it brings guidance. Sayyid Ahmad Khan also said that the Qur'an presented an image of the universe in which everything took place according to law. He upset many Muslims by insisting that the reward and punishment of sins would be the result of the natural working of law.

"There is one creator of all the universe, namely God. He is eternal . . . To believe that the reward and punishment of good and evil depends on the arbitrary command of God is absurd. The reward and punishment of good and evil depends on the laws of nature that have been established by God."[20]

[17] Sayyid Ahmad Khan, *Tahzibu-l-Akhlaq*, vol. 2, Lahore, Malik Fazlu-d-Din, 1870-1876, p. 6.

[18] For example note: Sayad Ahmad Khan Bahadur, *Review on Dr. Hunter's Indian Musalmans Are They Bound in Conscience To Rebel Against the Queen*, Lahore, Premier Book House, n.d.

[19] Sayyid Ahmad Khan, *Tafsiru-l-Qur'an*, vol. 1, pp. 37-39.

[20] *Tahzibu-l-Akhlaq*, vol. 2, pp. 170-172.

One of his reasons for advocating modern education was that Muslims ought to understand the working of natural law better. On the human plane, he assumed that the "natural" was the ability to discriminate between good and evil. Better education could also polish that faculty.

In seeking to understand the reasons for the rigidity of mind of the *ulema* of his age, Sayyid Ahmad Khan concluded that the original error had been a confusion between things of the spirit (*din*), and things of the world. In his view, true religion should always be carefully distinguished from worldly affairs. True religion, he said, is unchanging, but worldly affairs are always changing. Originally, the great *ulema* used their personal opinions to give judgments on worldly affairs. This was in itself, he says, a valid thing for them to have done. Later, however, these opinions on temporary issues became identified with unchanging truth. This meant, he says, that the *ulema* were considered law-givers in the same sense as the Qur'an; their human opinions became identified with the will of God.

In Sayyid Ahmad Khan's opinion, the unfortunate result of this process was that Islam became equated with *fiqh*, the personal opinions of the legists on worldly matters. This meant that *fiqh* became a rigid and unchanging system. Since it was considered a form of revelation, it was believed to be comprehensive. Muslims thought they had no need for any civil, criminal or trade code apart from this system. This belief was, in Sayyid Ahmad Khan's opinion, one of the major reasons for the decay of all the Muslim nations of the world at this time.[21]

Sayyid Ahmad Khan thus maintained that the original activities of the founders of the schools of law were a valid attempt to deal with the immediate problems of their age. The mistake came later when Muslims identified this temporary, limited group of opinions with fixed and immutable revelation. The fault of the *ulema* of Sayyid Ahmad Khan's age lay, in his opinion, in their unwillingness to re-examine their medieval code in the light of new problems.

In addition to his writings, Sayyid Ahmad Khan's energies were devoted to the founding and nourishing of a number of organizations devoted to the purpose of persuading Muslims to open themselves to the study of the many new ideas and problems that were impinging upon them. A Scientific Society for the introduction of western sciences was set up by him in 1864. In the same year, he founded a new modern school at Ghazipur, and he continued to encourage Muslims to establish educational committees for the purpose of studying their needs and creating new institutions.

His leadership qualities were remarkable. Most of the groups he set up functioned, and some of them published journals, worked at translating English materials into Urdu, and involved many different kinds of people in common tasks. Sayyid Ahmad Khan seems to have had a rare ability to stimulate con-

---

[21] *Ibid.*, pp. 140-142.

structive activity among his fellows. Many of the Muslim educators and writers who followed him acknowledged that he was the one to have urged them to do something. Even those who later differed from many of his religious views have acknowledged his leadership in this area.

Sayyid Ahmad Khan visited Europe in 1869-70. After his return, his main project, the establishment of a Muslim university, was realized. In 1878 college classes began at the new Anglo-Muhammadan Oriental College at Aligarh. It was intended to resemble Cambridge. The establishment of Aligarh meant that the Muslims generally had accepted Sayyid Ahmad Khan's fundamental thesis that they must educate themselves in contemporary knowledge.

His later enterprises included the founding of the Muhammadan Anglo-Oriental Educational Conference for the "general promotion of western education in Muslim India, for the enrichment of Urdu through translations of indispensable scientific works, to exercise political pressure for the acceptance of Urdu as the secondary language in all government and private schools, to emphasize the necessity for educating women as essential for the balanced intellectual development of future generations, and to formulate a policy for the higher education of Muslim students in Europe."[22]

His ideas on social and religious change were set forth in a journal, entitled *Tahzib al-Akhlaq*. Public interest was excited in this way, and although much controversy was also engendered, the result was to familiarize the Muslim community with the issues Sayyid Ahmad Khan wanted to raise.

On one basic issue he had to compromise. When Aligarh was established, Sayyid Ahmad Khan agreed to allow the traditionalists to conduct such religious training as was to be offered. A result has been that the universities before and after the establishment of Pakistan have not been centers in which religious ideas like those of Sayyid Ahmad Khan have been systematically debated. Such new ideas as have come forth have continued to emerge as a result of the efforts of individuals.

---

[22] Aziz Ahmad, *Islamic Modernism in India and Pakistan*, 1957-1964, London, Oxford University Press, 1967, p. 37, quoting the prospectus in Mawlawi Abd al-Haqq, *Sayyid Ahmad Khan*, 1959, pp. 138-139.

Muhammad Iqbal

THE second modernist to be discussed is Muhammad Iqbal (1873-1938). Iqbal's background was more simple than that of Sayyid Ahmad Khan. He was born in Sialkot, in the Punjab. His father was a small business man, a person influenced by traditional mysticism. As a young student, Iqbal early received attention because of his capacities as a poet with considerable lyrical power and noteworthy intelligence. One of the first teachers to help him was Shamsul Ulama Mir Hasen; he was a supporter of the revivalist activities that had been initiated by Sayyid Ahmad Khan in India, and stirred up in other parts of the Islamic world by Jamal al-Din al-Afghani.[1]

When Iqbal came to study in Lahore in 1895, he had as one of his professors Sir Thomas Arnold. Although we have no detailed information about relations between the two, we have a poem in which Iqbal expresses the affection he felt for his teacher.[2] Arnold, of all Western orientalists, was possibly the one most concerned to affirm the values of Islamic civilization, especially in terms of artistic works, and to expend energy gathering evidence to refute some of the more obvious Western misconceptions about Islam. His major work *The Preaching of Islam* is evidence of his perspective.[3] One can imagine that a westerner with such interests could well help strengthen the self-respect of his Muslim students. Also Arnold quite possibly helped Iqbal develop the attitude of balanced appreciation of western thought which remained characteristic of all his later writings about philosophy and religion.

The next phase of Iqbal's development was a period of three years' study in Europe. At Cambridge he worked with the famous neo-Hegelian J. M. E. McTaggart. From England, he went to Germany, where he worked at Heidelberg and Munich. To the latter university, he submitted for his doctorate a thesis entitled *The Development of Metaphysics in Persia*.

The work was a contribution to the history of religions since it brought to light some Persian Sufis who had been hitherto unknown in Europe. It also showed "a remarkable knowledge of European theology from Thomas Aquinas to Adolf von Harnack, and of German philosophical thought."[4]

After his return to Lahore in 1908, he did not move again except for very occasional visits elsewhere, until his death in 1938. He earned a living prac-

[1] Javid Iqbal, ed., *Stray Reflections*, Lahore, Sh. Ghulam Ali and Sons, 1961, pp. xv-xvii.

[2] Annamarie Schimmel, *Gabriel's Wing*, Leiden, Brill, 1963, p. 36.

[3] T. W. Arnold, *The Preaching of Islam*, (second edition), London, 1913.

[4] Schimmel, *Gabriel's Wing*, p. 38.

ticing law. On the side, he read omnivorously all the time; his library gives abundant evidence of his interests, and of his capacity to keep up to date with the latest thinking in all the areas of his concern. His friends say he was always reading. A book-dealer in Lahore says Iqbal kept him informed of what was being written in the West, and what must be ordered.[5]

Also, he wrote poetry in Urdu and Persian. There is nothing in the Muslim or the Western tradition that can quite be compared to Iqbal's poetic enterprises. In Lahore, poetry is a public activity, in the sense that there is a long tradition of regular, public reciting of poetry. Audience participation is immediate and responsive—cries of joy, sighs, and even tears are appropriate and normal responses to the poet's efforts. Iqbal was very conscious of this traditional heritage. He presented his writings in the usual manner, and was very aware of a need to excel in exactly the delicate skills of sound, appropriate imagery, and subtle suggestiveness that would elicit appreciative attention from connoisseurs. Possibly an artist more than any other man is bound to the past in that he knows the skill of those whose work he is attempting to surpass.

But Iqbal's poetry broke from the tradition radically in the matter of content. In part, the break came from giving a greatly increased significance to content as opposed to form as an end in itself. Further, the content was intended to change the hearts of the Muslim audience, and by means of that, to change the world. The poetry was an instrument for Iqbal's message to his fellow Muslims; a call to wake up, to focus on the real world, and to act. All of the poetry is related to this imperative to revive.

His other activities were similarly oriented around this core demand. We know of his maturity and originality as a philosopher of religion only by the chance that he was invited in 1928 to give a series of lectures at the universities of Hyderabad, Madras, and Aligarh. He had often indicated that he intended to write books on a number of subjects, but these lectures are all that we have of his systematic reasoning.[6] As with the poetry, there is nothing than can be compared to it, since it is an enterprise by a highly qualified man to do what no one else has done, namely to write, in the light of mid-twentieth-century knowledge, a discussion of the meaning and significance of fundamental Islamic values.

His third major sphere of activity was the political realm. He took part in a limited way in the affairs of his city and his province, and he kept very much up to date through his personal relationships with the major Muslim leaders of his time. His contribution was that of a man by nature "one who reflects." Yet no one of his community then or now seems to have found anything odd in the spectacle of a poet and philosopher serving as guide and confidant for the leaders of a movement for cultural independence. His intelligence and

[5] Reported by Javid Iqbal in conversation, 1960.

[6] Muhammad Iqbal, *The Reconstruction of Religious Thought in Islam*, London, Oxford University Press, 1934; reprinted Lahore, Ashraf, 1962.

acumen were evidently self-authenticating. On one of the occasions when he did speak formally, in 1930, he delivered an address to the Muslim League.[7] Although it is said that relatively few people heard it, or thought it of great significance at the time, that address has since been considered one of the major statements defining the attitude which led the Muslim League to fight for, and to get, Pakistan. He is considered a father of the nation; his tomb is placed at a location of much honor, right in front of the grand Bad Shahi mosque in Lahore.

Iqbal's political activities might be characterized as those of a self-appointed lobbyist. Having formulated his views, he continued to press them, especially informally, on the minds of men who respected him because of their love for his poetry, and their awe before his knowledge of Islamic religion and culture. Mohammed Ali Jinnah, who was to become Pakistan's first Governor General, kept Iqbal's letters.[8] From them, we can see the unfailing courtesy and kindliness of Iqbal's manner of giving guidance, as well as his purposefulness.

The Iqbalian perspective is a coherent whole that can be discerned throughout his writings: in the poetry, the philosophy, and the advice to politicians. His position as a posthumous founder of a nation means that certain concrete results of this perspective can also be observed.

The relationship between Iqbal's ideas and those of Sayyid Ahmad Khan is many-faceted. Both are committed to the survival of the community, and both are therefore directed towards discovering any flaws in the people's life-style that might stand in the way of that survival. Iqbal, living a generation later than Sayyid Ahmad Khan, was a part of a Muslim community for whom Western education had become accepted. He took this as given, and his efforts in advocating educational reform were rather directed towards insisting that a yet better mode of education would be one in which Muslims learned to know their own tradition in the light of contemporary knowledge. Iqbal had hoped to write a study of the history of Islamic law. His intention was that Muslims should know their own tradition more thoroughly than previous generations had, since new resources in research methods and materials were available. He once commented that he knew more about Aristotle than previous generations because of the resources now open to him.[9]

The Muslim community in Iqbal's time was distressed, not so much by one striking disaster, as had been the case with Sayyid Ahmad Khan, but by a range of increasingly difficult problems. A new dimension was disillusionment with the West, as a result of the wars and depressions of the twentieth century. Shortly before his death in 1938, Iqbal delivered the following speech over the radio to the people:

[7] Vahid, Syed Abdul, ed., *Thoughts and Reflections of Iqbal*, Lahore, Sh. Muhammad Ashraf, 1964, pp. 161 ff.

[8] *Letters of Iqbal to Jinnah*, Lahore, Sh. Muhammad Ashraf, 1942.

[9] Javid Iqbal, ed., *Stray Reflections*, p. 40.

"Today space and time are being annihilated and man is achieving success in unveiling the secrets of nature and harnessing its force to his own service. But in spite of all these developments, the tyranny of imperialism struts abroad, covering its face under the masks of Democracy, Nationalism, Communism, Fascism and heaven knows what else besides . . .

"As I look back on the year that has passed and as I look at the world in the midst of the New Year's rejoicings, it may be Abyssinia or Palestine, Spain or China, the same misery prevails in every corner of man's earthly home . . .

"Do you not see that the people of Spain, though they have the same common bond of one race, one nationality, one language and one religion, are cutting one another's throats and destroying their culture and civilization by their own hands owing to a difference in their economic creed? This one event shows clearly that national unity is not a very durable force. Only one unity is dependable, and that unity is the brotherhood of man, which is above race, nationality, colour or language.

"Let us therefore begin the New Year with the prayer that God Almighty may grant humanity to those who are in places of power and government and teach them to cherish mankind."[10]

Although Iqbal is rightly considered a founder of a nation, nevertheless his dislike for nationalism was a strong element in his thought. What he distrusted was the idea of a "nation as an end in itself"—this seemed to him one of the main sources of the rampaging violence of the age. Instead of idolatrous nationalism, he thought a healthy Muslim society must be one in which the goal was service. For him the phrases "vice-gerent of God on earth" and "servant of God" were the distinguishing characteristics of Muslims. The raison d'être of the Muslim community was to bear witness to God—to be a light to lighten the gentiles.

It would be incorrect to assume that Iqbal was advocating a new Muslim nation that would take exactly the shape that Pakistan took ten years after his death. The negotiations were delicate and complex during that period, and the leaders of the Muslim League might have agreed to a number of other possible options, such as, for instance, strong Muslim provinces within a federated India. Iqbal's emphasis had been on the need for a high degree of autonomy for Muslims. Such autonomy was thought of as essential to protect Muslim interests in a situation in which they were relatively backward as compared to Hindus in education, and to enable them to develop their own mode of modern educational and social institutions.

On the matter of the authority of the *ulema* and the Shari'ah, Iqbal's position resembled that of Sayyid Ahmad Khan, although the latter held a rather Newtonian view of the universe whereas the former thought more in a Whiteheadian fashion about a cosmos of unfolding process. This difference in cos-

---

[10] Vahid, Syed Abdul, ed., *Thoughts and Reflections of Iqbal*, pp. 374, 375.

mology meant that Sayyid Ahmad Khan thought "order" was more natural and easily attainable than Iqbal thought it was. Sayyid Ahmad Khan thought that sensible men could achieve order if they worked at it; Iqbal emphasized more strongly that men needed vision of ultimate ends as well as sense if their works were to be sound. The practical results of each position are, however, quite similar in that each required effort and thought from the members of the community.

Both of them thought the complacency of the traditionalists dangerous to the community because it might blind the people's eyes to the necessity of thought and action in such a way as to lead to the possible destruction of the community. In the Indian context, such destruction would have meant dropping to the bottom of the social scale. From such a perspective, the *ulema* could not be entrusted to advise on political and social matters, since they were not believed to have sufficient understanding of the present problems of the community. Sayyid Ahmad Khan and Iqbal both go further and challenge also the religious ideas of the traditionalists; both do so in the name of a more adequate knowledge of the tradition.

Iqbal argued that the closing of the doors of independent reasoning in matters of law and social practice had taken place in Islamic society in response to the Mongol invasions. He wrote:

"On top of all this came the destruction of Baghdad—the centre of Muslim intellectual life—in the middle of the thirteenth century. This was indeed a great blow, and all the contemporary historians of the invasion of the Tartars describe the havoc of Baghdad with a half-suppressed pessimism about the future of Islam. For fear of further disintegration, which is only natural in such a period of political decay, the conservative thinkers of Islam focussed all their efforts on the one point of preserving a uniform social life for the people by a jealous exclusion of all innovations in the law of Sharia as expounded by the early doctors of Islam. Their leading idea was social order, and there is no doubt that they were partly right, because organization does to a certain extent counteract the forces of decay. But they did not see, and our modern Ulema do not see, that the ultimate fate of a people does not depend so much on organization as on the worth and power of individual men . . . Thus a false reverence for past history and its artificial resurrection constitute no remedy for a people's decay."[11]

Iqbal thus sees all the tendencies to assert that Islamic legal and social patterns are immutable to be a result of one unfortunate phase of Islamic history. The triumphant early period was not characterized by any such narrow view, and survival in the present requires a return to openness. Iqbal wrote:

"Turning now to the groundwork of legal principles in the Qur'an, it is perfectly clear that far from leaving no scope for human thought and legislative

<hr />

[11] Muhammad Iqbal, *The Reconstruction of Religious Thought in Islam*, p. 151.

activity the intensive breadth of these principles virtually acts as an awakener of human thought. Our early doctors of law taking their cue mainly from this groundwork evolved a number of legal systems; and the student of Mohammedan history knows very well that nearly half the triumphs of Islam as a social and political power were due to the legal acuteness of these doctors. 'Next to the Romans' says Von Kremer, 'there is no other nation besides the Arabs which could call its own a system of law so carefully worked out.' But with all their comprehensiveness, these systems are after all individual interpretations, and as such cannot claim any finality."[12]

Iqbal's position is sometimes characterized as *"ijma'"* modernism. He discussed the matter as follows:

"The third source of Mohammaden law is Ijma, which is in my opinion, perhaps the most important legal notion of Islam. It is, however, strange that this important notion, while invoking great academic discussions in early Islam, remained practically a mere idea, and rarely assumed the form of a permanent institution in any Mohammedan country . . . The transfer of the power of Ijtihad from individual representatives of schools to a Muslim legislative assembly which . . . is the only possible form Ijma can take in modern times will secure contributions to legal discussion from laymen who happen to possess a keen insight into affairs. In this way alone we can stir into activity the dormant spirit of life in our legal system, and give it an evolutionary outlook."[13]

Ijtihad means independent judgment, and *ijma'* means consensus. Iqbal is arguing that the idea of decision-making on matters concerning the community by means of some form of representative institution was present from the beginning of Islamic history. He maintains that those who held actual power, rulers who dominated for centuries because they controlled the military, preferred to leave "consensus" and thinking about legal and social matters in the hands of a few scholars. Thus the founding principles of Islam had not been fully implemented because various kinds of corruption prevented the proper realization of the ideals.

One way to consider this issue might be to see it as an instance of debate between what some Western scholars would identify as "priestly" and "prophetic" strains in a religious tradition. Iqbal himself has acknowledged the usefulness of the priestly strain, especially in a time of collapse such as followed the Mongol invasions. He recognizes the importance of continuance of customary practices as a means of unifying the community. Indeed, he feared the danger of a kind of liberalism that might destroy all the unifying bonds. He commented:

"We heartily welcome the liberal movement in modern Islam; but it must also be admitted that the appearance of liberal ideas in Islam constitutes also the most critical moment in the history of Islam. Liberalism has a tendency to act

---

[12] *Ibid.*, p. 168.
[13] *Ibid.*, pp. 173, 174.

as a force of disintegration and the race-idea, which appears to be working in modern Islam with greater force than ever, may ultimately wipe off the broad human outlook which Muslim people have imbibed from the religion. . . ."[14]

In our earlier discussion of Iqbal's comments on the Spanish civil war, we indicated something of his deep uneasiness about secular nationalism. He was very aware that Muslims were being driven by forces of economic and social change towards forms of secular nationalism like those of Europe, as in the case of Turkey, and he distrusted these developments profoundly. The relationship he discerned between secular nationalism and racism was perhaps particularly evident to an Indian Muslim, since the Indians had experienced much more racial arrogance on the part of the British as British power over India had increased. In the sixteenth century, the Europeans in India were much less racist than were their nineteenth-century counterparts. As Iqbal died before European secular nationalism reaped its harvest in the Second World War, we should perhaps acknowledge his perceptiveness.

Iqbal was much more deeply concerned than Sayyid Ahmad Khan had been to insist that changes should be made in Muslim ways of life only after the possible consequences of such changes had been weighed with the utmost care. The criterion for him was whether such changes could reasonably be expected to further the implementation of the ideals of which the Muslim community was the guardian. If, for instance, new political ideals would militate against the ideals of brotherhood, Iqbal would have opposed them. He wrote as follows:

"The spirit of man in its forward movement is restrained by forces which seem to be working in the opposite direction. This is only another way of saying that life moves with the weight of its own past on its back, and that in any view of social change the value and function of the forces of conservatism cannot be lost sight of . . . Islam is non-territorial in its character, and its aim is to furnish a model for the final combination of humanity by drawing its adherents from a variety of mutually repellent races, and then transforming this atomic aggregate into a people possessing a self-consciousness of their own."[15]

Iqbal conceived of the community as the bearer of ideals. The unity of the community was therefore essential if the ideals were to remain alive. Changes, even small changes in apparently minor matters, were suspect if they threatened to upset the unity of the people. Iqbal is not easy to tie down to specific examples on matters of this kind because he was continually involved in arguing against those who wanted to retain the medieval way of life intact, and in more or less the same breath arguing against those who wanted to change so fast and so much that nothing discernibly Islamic would remain. The key to understanding him lies in recognizing that for him the struggle was to keep alive a vision of the good while at the same time implementing as much of that vision as was possible in the present. Every decision had to be weighed in the

[14] *Ibid.*, pp. 162,163.
[15] *Ibid.*, pp. 166,167.

light of ultimate goodness and justice. His advice to those concerned with trying to redesign Muslim institutions was as follows:

"In the evolution of such a society even the immutability of socially harmless rules relating to eating and drinking, purity or impurity, has a life-value of its own . . . The critic of these institutions must therefore try to secure, before he undertakes to handle them, a clear insight into the ultimate significance of the social experiment embodied in Islam. He must look at their structure, not from the standpoint of social advantage or disadvantage to this or that country, but from the point of view of the larger purpose which is being gradually worked out in the life of mankind as a whole."[16]

From this perspective, the priestly is secondary to the prophetic, since the original insight into God's purpose derives from prophetic experience. Iqbal describes prophecy as follows:

"The mystic does not wish to return from the repose of 'unitary experience'; and even when he does return, as he must, his return does not mean much for mankind at large. The prophet's return is creative. He returns to insert himself in the sweep of time with a view to control the forces of history, and thereby to create a fresh world of ideals. . . . Another way of judging the value of a prophet's religious experience therefore, would be to examine the types of manhood that he has created and the cultural world that has sprung out of the spirit of his Message."[17]

The finality of Muhammad's prophethood lies in the realm of the perfection of the perspective transmitted through him. The argument in Iqbal's day between himself and the traditionalists revolved around the definition of "what" was transmitted. For the traditionalists a comprehensive life-system had been passed on; faithfulness consisted of dutiful adherence to unchanging patterns. For Iqbal, the "spirit of the message" was a dynamism from which had followed the birth of inductive intellect, the abolition of castes of priests, and the destruction of hereditary kingship. To manifest that spirit in the present would mean to exhibit comparable world-transforming energy and intelligence.

Iqbal discussed the relationship between past and present vision in his poem *The Mosque of Cordoba.*

"Yet, in this frame of things, gleams of immortal life
Show where some servant of God wrought into some high shape
Work whose perfection is still bright with the splendor of Love—
Love, the well-spring of life. . ."[18]

"Servant of God" in Iqbal's terminology means someone whose works bear witness to God, mirroring His attributes. Thus the more devout the service, the more creative the work. The modern Muslim should derive from contemplation of the works of Muslims of earlier centuries insight into how fruitful

---

[16] *Ibid.*, p. 167.
[17] *Ibid.*, pp. 124-125.
[18] V. G. Kiernan, trans., *Poems from Iqbal*, London, John Murray, 1955, p. 38.

God-centered vision can be. The communication of such vision across centuries can not mean a literal reproduction of the same masterpiece, since then the art would be unreal. The more profound the influence of earlier centuries, the more original a new work should be, if vision has genuinely been transmitted. The "love" that is the well-spring of life creates new life.

Iqbal thinks that Muslim experts on jurisprudence, economists, designers of new social institutions, parliamentarians, and so forth should all be creative in their own spheres. Their works also should mirror God's attributes, for example justice and mercy. Creativeness is the main virtue upheld and continually discussed by Iqbal. By contrast, Sayyid Ahmad Khan, though a notably creative man, had not laid similar emphasis on this quality. Sayyid Ahmad Khan tended more to talk of hard work and humility as primary virtues.

Iqbal's radical ideas about personality were first brought to the attention of Muslims in his poem *Secrets of the Self*.[19] He used the imagery of Persian mystical poetry to attack traditional forms of self-negating mysticism. Such self-negation was dangerous to the community since it could breed other-worldliness, and passivity in the fact of challenge. Self-negation, Iqbal insisted, was bad religion. Good religion was to affirm the strengthening of individuality. A strengthened individual would be increasingly creative. Such creativeness would bring the individual closer to God, Himself the source of creative freedom. Thus growth towards God, polishing the heart so that the divine attributes could be reflected in its mirror, was not a matter of destroying characteristics of individuality, but of strengthening true individuality.

What needed to be destroyed within persons were forces of fear, self-doubt, self-contempt and all the anxieties that prohibited the bursting forth of genuine and daring individuality. Abraham was a model often used by Iqbal to characterize authentic faith—to leap forward, to abandon the known, to follow a promise not yet realized. Such was authentic faith.

"Faith is like Abraham at the stake: to be Self-honouring and God-drunk, is faith. Hear me."[20]

Iqbal takes the Qur'anic verse as his source:

"Verily, God will not change the condition of men, till they change what is in themselves."[21]

Again, in the words of the poet-philosopher:

"If he does not take the initiative, if he does not evolve the inner richness of his being, if he ceases to feel the inward push of advancing life, then the spirit within him turns into stone and he is reduced to the level of dead matter."[22]

---

[19] R. A. Nicholson, trans., *The Secrets of the Self*, London, Macmillan, 1920. (Lahore, 1955).

[20] V. G. Kiernan, trans., *Poems from Iqbal*, p. 36.

[21] Qur'an 13:12. Quoted in the *Reconstruction* Lectures, p. 12.

[22] Muhammad Iqbal, *The Reconstruction of Religious Thought in Islam*, p. 12.

Freedom is a necessary condition of goodness:

"Goodness is not a matter of compulsion; it is the Self's free surrender to the moral ideal and arose out of willing co-operation of free egos. A being whose movements are wholly determined cannot produce goodness."[23]

Within a condition of freedom, the strengthening of individuality is a continuous process. Iqbal explicitly insisted that no possible end to such a process could be envisioned by a creative man.

> "What can I do? My nature is averse to rest;
> My heart is impatient like the breeze in the poppy field;
> When the eye beholds an object of beauty
> The heart yearns for something more beautiful still;
> From the spark to the star, from the star to the sun
> Is my quest;
> I have no desire for a goal,
> For me, rest spells death!
> With an impatient eye and a hopeful heart
> I seek for the end of that which is endless!"[24]

In the lectures, *The Reconstruction of Religious Thought in Islam*, he devotes an entire chapter to a discussion of "The Human Ego—His Freedom and Immortality." The concluding paragraph reads as follows:

"However, according to the teaching of the Quran, the ego's re-emergence brings him a 'sharp sight' (950:21) whereby he clearly sees his self-built 'fate fastened round his neck.' Heaven and Hell are states not localities. The descriptions in the Quran are visual representations of an inner fact, i.e. character. Hell, in the words of the Quran, is God's kindled fire which mounts above the hearts'—the painful realization of one's failure as a man. Heaven is the joy of triumph over the forces of disintegration. There is no such thing as eternal damnation in Islam. The word 'eternity' used in certain verses, relating to Hell, is explained by the Quran itself to mean only a period of time (78:23). Time cannot be wholly irrelevant to the development of personality. Character tends to become permanent; its reshaping must require time. Hell, therefore, as conceived by the Quran, is not a pit of everlasting torture inflicted by a revengeful God; it is a corrective experience which may make a hardened ego once more sensitive to the living breeze of Divine Grace. Nor is Heaven a holiday. Life is one and continuous. Man marches always onward to receive ever fresh illuminations from an Infinite Reality which 'every moment appears in a new glory.' And the recipient of Divine illumination is not merely a passive recipient. Every act of a free ego creates a new situation, and thus offers further opportunities of creative unfolding."[25]

---

[23] *Ibid.*, p. 85.

[24] K. G. Saiyidain, *Iqbal's Educational Philosophy*, Lahore, Sh. Muhammad Ashraf, 6th edition, 1965, p. 36, quoting *Payim-i-Mashriq*, pp. 148-149.

[25] Muhammad Iqbal, *The Reconstruction of Religious Thoughts in Islam*, p. 123.

Iqbal has sometimes been accused of advocating a Nietzschean superman as the model for his people. Although it is true that much of Nietzsche's thinking interested him, especially the attacks on passivity, it is also true that he himself thought Nietzsche's perspective limited.

"We can aspire only for what is absolutely new, and the absolutely new is unthinkable in Nietzsche's view which is nothing more than a Fatalism. . . . Such a doctrine far from keying up the human organism for the fight of life, tends to destroy its action-tendencies and relaxes the tension of the ego."[26]

The perfect man, the superman, the *mu'min*—these and other terms are regularly used by Iqbal to point to the ideal he envisaged—the individual continually strengthening his creative powers. The *mu'min* is a Qur'anic term used to refer to a believer whose faith is more certain and distinctive than that of many other members of the community. Faith in the traditional Islamic perspective is not a characteristic that can be measured exactly, but there is recognition that it is more actively present in some than in others. Resolution of the issue of evaluating faith has been left to God. Iqbal's position on this matter is traditional in that he is not suggesting any institutionalized method of measuring faith.

The "Perfect Man" is a term that has been widely used by Muslim mystics for centuries. It is usually linked by images connected with the idea of polishing the mirror of the heart so that the divine attributes may be reflected to the darkened world. Iqbal uses the same images, with the significant difference we have noted, namely that for him the polishing of the heart is not self-negating, but affirming of the qualities of creative individuality. He therefore has a "superman" idea only in the sense that all men have capacities to overcome fear and passivity, and to transform themselves into strong individuals. But the strength advocated is a strength disciplined by submission to God. Such submission means overcoming all in the self that is contrary or hostile to the divine attributes—such as meanness, defensiveness against other persons, self-contempt and self-centredness. In Iqbal's terms, a strong heart is a generous heart, able and ready to spend itself in service.

> "Lo, like a candle wrestling with the night
> O'er my own self I pour my flooding tears.
> I spent my self, that there might be more light,
> More loveliness, more joy for other men.
> Not for one moment takes my ardent breast
> Repose from burning;"[27]

To spend the self—to give energy, will, and concentrated attention, is not the same as self-denial or negation. Iqbal's quarrel with traditional Sufism was

[26] *Ibid.*, p. 116.
[27] Arthur J. Arberry, trans., *The Mysteries of Selflessness*, London, John Murray, 1953, p. 13.

over this distinction. One could call him a critical mystic. The source of his criticism of self-negating mysticism was his certainty of the truth of his own intimations of the Divine nature and purpose.

Sayyid Ahmad Khan is usually thought of as a rationalist because of his endeavors to prove the reasonableness of his religion. As we noted, he saw the point of contact between man and God in man's conscience, and ability to discern "the natural." On the other hand, Iqbal appears to be deliberately anti-rational. Especially in the poetry, he regularly appears to disparage reason. Consider, for example, his poem entitled *Modern Man*:

> "*Love fled, Mind stung him like a snake*; he could not
>   Force it to vision's will.
> He tracked the orbits of the stars, yet could not
>   Travel his own thoughts' world;
> Entangled in the labyrinth of his science
>   Lost count of good and ill;
> Took captive the sun's rays, and yet no sunrise
>   On life's thick night unfurled."[28]

The limitations of reason, in Iqbal's view, lie in the area of stimulating vision. Sayyid Ahmad Khan did not see vision as a primary need for his life-situation, but for Iqbal it was the central problem. The difference is partly a matter of a changed perspective on modern man; Iqbal published the volume containing this poem in 1936. He conceived of modern man as a stung, writhing and tormented being. Iqbal did not believe in nature as Sayyid Ahmad Khan had done. Man, from the poet's vantage point, appeared estranged from his nature. Undisciplined reason had contributed to that estrangement, inasmuch as it had deluded him into thinking he understood when he did not, and had given him a false sense of his power because of his conquests over matter.

Love always takes priority over reason in Iqbal's thought, since love alone can give the vision which can properly direct reason. "Love" in this context is translated from an Urdu word, *ishq*, with Persian and Arabic usage behind it. Other instances of Iqbal's references to *ishq* are as follows:

> "Love is Gabriel's breath, Love is Mahomed's strong heart,
> Love is the envoy of God, Love the utterance of God.
> Even our mortal clay, touched by Love's ecstasy, glows:
> Love is a new-pressed wine, Love is the goblet of kings,
> Love is the priest of the shrine, Love the commander of hosts,
> Love the son of the road, counting a thousand homes."[29]

---

[28] V. G. Kiernan, *Poems from Iqbal*, p. 66. Italicization of the first words is the translator's.

[29] *Ibid.*, p. 38.

This Islamic sense of love implies a quality which touches man—Gabriel's breath—and stirs him out of his uncreative state into generous strength— Muhammad's strong heart. When it touches man, it leads him to transcend his limited condition. As compared to Christian ideas, this quality of love might be rather like grace, or the Holy Spirit. The wind bloweth where it listeth. Love, the son of the road.

Iqbal is more concerned to describe the fruits of "being touched by love" than to discuss where the love comes from, or what the manner of its travel is. But inasmuch as the Mosque of Cordoba can stir up love in Iqbal, so also can love be transmitted among men by example. The past is therefore a storehouse of seeds which have the present and future potential of engendering creative individuality in the hearts of men. The instruments or seeds of love are many. A good poetic image might be one. The record of a good life might be another. An historical event like the ending of hereditary kingship is also a possibility. The works of Iqbal are full of references to such seeds. But, of course, problems as to what soil the seeds fall into are also present.

The poem which followed *The Secrets of the Self* was entitled *The Mysteries of Selflessness*. Here Iqbal argued for the necessity of life in the community as a discipline to shape the development of the self.

> "   He who has not drunk
> The water of the People's sacred well,
> The flames of minstrelsy within his lute
> Grow cold, and die. The Individual
> Alone, is heedless of high purposes"[30]

The breath that stires up creativeness is response to concerns that are not self-centered. From this perspective, it follows that strong individuality is possible only in one capable of forgetting about himself as he expends his efforts attempting to solve problems and to serve people outside himself. Even a poet, in Iqbal's view, will only keep his powers if he is engaged in commitment to the needs of other people, and in service to high purposes. Iqbal himself undoubtedly kept his lyrical power to the very end.

But membership in the Muslim community is of particular importance since only there can the highest purposes be discovered. The community exists to bear witness to the unity of God. Membership in it entails responsibility to witness.

> "If thou a Muslim art,
> Till all the world proclaims the Name of God
> Thou canst not rest one moment. Knowest thou not
> The verse in Holy Scripture, calling thee
> To be *a people just, God's witnesses?*
> . . .

---

[30] Arthur J. Arberry, trans., *The Mysteries of Selflessness*, p. 6.

Life here below is bound up with his Faith
None can survive, save guarded by his Law.
Having his Book beneath thy arm, stride out
With greater boldness to the battlefield
Of works; for human thought, idolatrous
And idol-fashioning, is all the time
In quest of some new image; in these days
It follows once again old Azar's trade,
And man creates an ever novel god
Whose joy is shedding blood, whose hallowed name
Is Color, Fatherland, Blood-Brotherhood.
Humanity is slaughtered like a sheep
Before this worthless idol. Thou whose lips
Have touched the sacred bowl of Abraham,
Whose blood is ardent with his holy wine,
Against this falsehood, garmented as truth,
Lift now the blade. *There is not aught but God*
And smite!"[31]

What causes man continually to thwart the manifestation of God's attributes of justice and unity? The devil, as might be expected. Man needs the community of the faithful in part for support and strengthening against demonic whispering. The devil is a vivid and complex figure in Iqbal's poetry. Shaytan (Satan), as he is called, is necessary as a stimulus to struggle.

"Error, which may be ascribed as a kind of intellectual evil is an indispensable factor in the building up of experience."[32]

For Iqbal, paradise is the state of non-individuation. Since he considers individuation to be the greatest good, he believes that Satan serves a constructive purpose. Satan jolts man into authentic existence. Satan also represents in Iqbal's later poems the political forces in the modern world that work against the manifestation of love on earth.

"*Satan*

I it was
Who drew in Europe's brain the fantasy
Of Empire, I who snapped the spell of mosque
Of church, of temple; I who taught the homeless
That all is ruled by Fate, and filled their guardians
With capitalism's hot frenzy."[33]

---

[31] *Ibid.*, pp. 54, 55. Translator's italics.
[32] Muhammad Iqbal, *The Reconstruction of Religious Thought in Islam*, p. 87.
[33] V. G. Kiernan, *Poems from Iqbal*, p. 79.

Iqbal was fascinated by the figure of the devil. He felt evil as an immediate reality, challenging, life-giving, threatening, and deadly. His poems point to manifestations of evil in a great variety of shapes, sometimes useful, sometimes life-destroying. The good side of the devil is seen to be his contribution to the creative vitality of man.

> "*Satan*
>
> But in Man's pinch of dust my daring spirit has
>   breathed ambition
> The warp and woof of mind and reason are woven
>   of my sedition . . . . .
> Ask this of God, when next you stand alone
>   within His sight—
> Whose blood is it has painted Man's long history
>   so bright?"[34]

Sometimes Iqbal sees the devil as an instrument in the mysterious purposes of God. In one poem, Satan speaks to God as follows:

> "If I would not kneel to him
> The cause was Your own fore-ordaining will."[35]

The implication seems to be that Iqbal believes that God approves of the restless creativeness of man, and that the rebellion of Satan was somehow fore-ordained in order to provide a spur to man's discovery of his creative powers. On the other hand, sometimes Iqbal pictures Satan as the enemy of those men who devote themselves in single-minded faithfulness to God.

> "*Satan to his Political Offspring*
> The man who famine-racked still fears no death—
> Mahomed's spirit from his breast expel!"[36]

The devil for Iqbal is thus both life-giving and life-destroying. He is the greatest ally, and the greatest enemy of man.

Iqbal's ideas about God are similarly complex. Sayyid Ahmad Khan, although he had conceived of God as transcendent, had yet thought of the divine-human relation as natural, requiring of man sincerity and dutifulness. In Iqbal's thought, there is more of a suggestion that man must take an unnatural leap in order to reach God; hence the prevalence of the image of Abraham in his writings. Prayer was an effort to transcend a situation of absence.

"Prayer . . . is an expression of man's inner yearning for a response in the

---

[34] *Ibid.*, pp. 52, 53.
[35] *Ibid.*, p. 64.
[36] *Ibid.*, p. 74.

awful silence of the universe. It is a unique process of discovery whereby the searching ego affirms itself in the very moment of self-negation, and thus discovers its own worth and justification as a dynamic factor in the life of the universe."[37]

As compared to Sayyid Ahmad Khan, Iqbal tended to think of the universe as empty of support for man. The greater feeling of alienation exemplified in Iqbal may be partly explained by his post-Einstein understanding of the complexity of the cosmos as contrasted with the simpler Newtonian ideas of Sayyid Ahmad Khan. However, one would not tend to suggest that when a Westerner like Kafka writes about alienation he is motivated largely by problems concerned with theories about the size of the universe. Iqbal's agony, like Kafka's, is the fruit of a situation of despair—despair because no answer comes to cries for meaning, hope, and justice.

Iqbal's greater despair seems to us a measure of the change in the condition of the community as over against the rest of the world. There seemed to be much less hope of achieving economic and social equality with Western nations. Also, the Western nations appeared less admirable as guides and models for a new world, partly as a result of the exhibition of savagery they put on in 1914-1918. The Muslim community was thus perceived as weak and despairing in the face of a corrupt stronger power. In all this, there seemed little indication that Muslim man could find from God the hope and direction he required.

Nevertheless, Iqbal conceived of the leap as possible. Creativeness was proof for him of this possibility. The creative man, by transcending himself, and giving birth to the new, came closer to God. In the *Reconstruction* lectures, God is spoken of as the Ultimate Ego.

"The characteristic of the ego is spontaneity . . . The Ultimate Ego that makes the emergent emerge is immanent in nature, and is described by the Qur'an as the 'First and the Last, the visible and the invisible.' "[38]

God is, from Iqbal's perspective, a free Creator.

"His 'I-amness' is independent, elemental, absolute. Of such a self it is impossible for us to form an adequate conception . . . The Ultimate Ego exists in pure duration wherein change ceases to be a succession of varying attitudes, and reveals its true character as continuous creation, 'untouched by weariness and unseizable by slumber or sleep' . . . Reality is a rationally directed creative life. To interpret this life as an ego is not to fashion God after the image of man. It is only to accept the simple fact of experience that life is not a formless fluid, but an organizing principle of unity, a synthetic activity which holds together and focalizes the dispersing dispositions of the living organism for a constructive purpose. The operation of thought which is essentially symbolic in character veils the true nature of life, and can only picture it as a kind

---

[37] Muhammad Iqbal, *The Reconstruction of Religious Thought in Islam*, p. 92.
[38] *Ibid.*, pp. 106, 107.

of universal current flowing through all things. . . . But we have a first hand knowledge of the appreciative aspect of life from within. Intuition reveals life as a centralizing ego."[39]

It is not easy to be sure one has grasped all the meaning Iqbal attributes to intuition. It is like the love, *ishq*, which we discussed earlier; it transcends reason; it is prayer; it is a self-transcending leap. It glimpses purpose, but a particular purpose is not final, since, in the unfolding of time, each particular purpose is transcended.

Iqbal, in spite of his anti-Sufi attitudes, nevertheless considers inner spiritual experience an ultimate key to the reality of God. He differs from some earlier Sufis, however, in his insistence that nature and history are also valid sources of knowledge. He says that the Qur'an urged Muslims to take the material world, and history, seriously. Knowledge from the outside and knowledge from the inside should support each other in a properly oriented, self-concentrated individual. The community in a time of stress like the present has great need of such individuals.

"The only effective power, therefore, is the rearing of self-concentrated individuals. Such individuals alone reveal the depth of life. They disclose new standards in the light of which we begin to see that our environment is not wholly inviolable and requires revision."[40]

The situation of the self-concentrated individual is paradoxical in that he is moving towards an eternity of ever-increasing individuation, and yet also coming to know with greater intimacy the Ultimate Ego.

The glimpse of God should transform the man who sees.

> "I sowed my eye into the field of love
> And reaped a harvest of vision"[41]

But, since this process of receiving vision, which leads on to self-transcendence, is unceasing, the end cannot be the final liberation of the self by absorption into the divine. Iqbal is thus in the Sufi tradition in his insistence on the importance of intuitive knowledge, but he does not conclude either that other sources of knowledge, such as nature and history, are useless, or that the man who had the vision ought to follow that vision into the absolute destruction of the being he formerly was. He rather conceives of the vision-receiving self as one who transcends his former self by becoming a more focussed and coherent individual. And the more coherent he is, the more he can transform his world.

Since Iqbal believes that authentic response to God strengthens genuine individuality, he also believes that a community made up of such men ought to be powerful. The Muslim community is the one in which brotherhood has been upheld as a goal, and in which idolatry has been condemned. It ought

---

[39] *Ibid.*, pp. 56-61.
[40] *Ibid.*, p. 151.
[41] Annemarie Schimmel, *Gabriel's Wing*, p. 131.

therefore to be more possible for Muslims than for others to make concrete the vision that they have of a community directed towards making real among men the Divine attributes of justice and goodness. Iqbal calls for self-concentrated individuals who will make clear to the community its responsibilities in the present. These responsibilities include regaining power, but also going further, and becoming a model for other nations. In this respect, he was asking more of the community than Sayyid Ahmad Khan had done. The latter wanted to regain a position of respect, but he did not urge a messianic role as strongly as Iqbal did.

If God's purposes are continually unfolding, how can it be said that Muhammad's prophethood was final? Iqbal devoted several pages of the Reconstruction lectures to this problem.

"The prophet of Islam seems to stand between the ancient and the modern world. In so far as the source of his revelation is concerned, he belongs to the ancient world; in so far as the spirit of his revelation is concerned, he belongs to the modern world. In him life discovers other sources of knowledge suitable to its new direction. The birth of Islam . . . is the birth of inductive intellect. In Islam prophecy reaches its perfection in discovering the need of its own abolition."[42]

Iqbal believes that the Qur'an urged man to study nature and history. For him, the finality of Prophethood means that man from now on must be thrown back on his own resources in order to achieve full self-consciousness.

"The abolition of priesthood and hereditary kingship in Islam, the constant appeal to reason and experience in the Qur'an, and the emphasis that it lays on Nature and history as sources of human knowledge, are all different aspects of the same idea of finality."[43]

One might say the stage had been set for man to achieve his individuality, free from the oppression of tyrannical kings or false religions.

But if the aim is a free self increasing its creative powers, what need is there for religion? Since Iqbal entitled the last chapter of his Reconstruction lectures "Is Religion Possible?" he obviously saw this question too. His answer is that the most intense and self-transcending experience possible is a religious one. Also only such experiences can make man capable of that kind of virtuous action which is necessary if men are to become capable of responsible corporate life.

"And religion, which in its higher manifestations is neither dogma, nor priesthood, nor ritual, can alone ethically prepare the modern man for the burden of the great responsibility which the advancement of modern science necessarily involves, and restore to him that attitude of faith which makes him capable of winning a personality here and retaining it hereafter."[44]

---

[42] Muhammad Iqbal, *The Reconstruction of Religious Thought in Islam*, p. 126.
[43] *Ibid.*, p. 126.
[44] *Ibid.*, p. 189.

This intuitive reaching for contact with God is characterized by Iqbal as natural.

"Thus the experience reached is a perfectly natural experience and possesses a biological significance of the highest importance to the ego. It is the human ego rising higher than mere reflection, and mending its transiency by appropriating the eternal. . . The final act is not an intellectual act, but a vital act which deepens the whole being of the ego, and sharpens his will with the creative assurance that the world is not something to be merely seen, or known through concepts but something to be made and re-made by continuous action."[45]

The phrase "appropriating the eternal" is significant here. The individual who becomes more individualized through his religious experiences, also becomes more God-like in that he appropriates the Divine attributes. Creativeness itself is one such attribute. Iqbal's messianism has its roots partly in this idea. The community made up of men who have appropriated the Divine attributes must necessarily manifest those attributes to the world. The more creative they are, the more God-like, and the greater the responsibility to bear witness. This might be dangerous doctrine if it were not rooted in the idea that authentic mystical experience must bear the fruits of the attributes the community had always recognized as true—justice and mercy among them. Anything else, from Iqbal's perspective, would not be genuine creativeness or religion.

[45] *Ibid.*, pp. 197, 198.

Ghulam Ahmad Parwez

THE third modernist under discussion is Ghulam Ahmad Parwez (1903-). A retired civil servant, he is the leader of a group of Pakistani Muslims who call their organization Idarah Tulu'l Islam (the "Dawn of Islam" circle, a title taken from a poem by Iqbal). The publication of the group's journal began in 1938 in Delhi. Publication of the journal ceased in 1942, and was resumed in 1948 from Karachi. Parwez himself has published a number of books in Urdu, and a few pamphlets in English. He has contributed regularly to the journal. In 1957 he was appointed a member of the Islamic Law Commission, but that group ceased to exist after the 1958 *coup d'état*. The Tulu'l Islam movement holds weekly open public meetings, which are often addressed by Parwez.

The background of Parwez is not different in any significant respect from that of many others of his generation who attended colleges in India, got jobs as minor civil servants, and spent most of their lives in that profession. He is a kind of representative white-collar worker, and representative product of the new educational methods. His personality hardly obtrudes at all in his writings except perhaps in the striking urge to systematize. The main influences on him are not those of teachers or friends, as in the case of the earlier modernists, but rather the writings of the modernists. He takes many ideas from Sayyid Ahmad Khan and Iqbal. When he differs from them, he is moved by an obvious impatience. He wants solutions to the problems of the present generation, and although the earlier modernists offered much that he agrees with, he yet feels the need of much more definite planning and instruction than he finds in their writings. It is perhaps relevant that the first two had distinguished Westerners as their personal friends, whereas such is not the case with Parwez. But most white-collar workers do not have distinguished friends, or occasions to travel. The very absence of the spectacular or the distinctive in the experience of Parwez is a quality that makes his writings an important clue to the state of mind of Pakistanis like him.

Although it has been estimated that no more than three thousand subscribe to the Tulu'l Islam journal, Parwez is known to a much wider audience than that. Such notoriety as he has achieved can be attributed mainly to the fact that in the Pakistani context he has served as one of the main opponents of the traditionalist religious leaders. He carries on his arguments with them at the level of pamphleteering and abuse-hurling. Probably most of the educated elite, especially in civil service and military circles have heard about him by his nickname, "Denier of Hadith." Pakistan, like most societies, is a place where many people who do not read a man's books have yet heard about him, and have some impression of his ideas.

Despite his age, Parwez has a number of characteristics that make him appear very contemporary. Some of his most interesting writings have been letters addressed to imaginary young men and women. The latter are presumed to be the products of a westernized form of education, contemptuous of the less educated religious leaders, and anxious to find guidance for the creation of a new world in which they can retain both their national pride and the values of an industrialized society. The imaginary young man is named Selim, and the imaginary young woman Tahirah.

In using a quotation from Iqbal as the name for his movement, and in his numerous references to the poet in all his writings, Parwez manifests a clear intention to claim that his message is a new version of the imperatives of the poet. One gains from his writings, therefore, an idea of what happened in one instance as the next generation tried to make sense of Iqbal's legacy. There are, of course, numerous other groups and individuals in Pakistan and in India who are attempting to articulate Iqbal's ideas. Parwez is not in any notable sense a distinguished interpreter of Iqbal. His claim to our interest lies rather in his role as an exponent of one new form of modernism.

The problem central to Parwez' writing is the issue of how to make the new nation of Pakistan powerful and successful. Since Selim and Tahirah are citizens of the new nation, they want guidance as to what immediate steps they should take. Parwez tells them that the religious leaders are basic obstacles to the creation of a new and prosperous Pakistan. He says that the religious leaders care nothing for the problems of the poor; they are only yes men for the rich landlords. In his letters to Selim, he tells a number of anecdotes about situations in which the poor cried for help, but the *ulema* ignored them, and went about their traditional business of administering religious service for the comfort of the rich. For example:

"A poor woman is pictured huddled by the stove with her hungry and shivering baby; her husband comes home despondent, still unable to find work and to feed his family. At the same time, in the Mosque, a rich man presents an expensive carpet for the people to pray on.

"In another family, a starving boy comes home from school, and finds no food. At the same time, in a rich man's house, a feast is being held to celebrate the first fast of the rich man's son."[1]

Parwez' attack on the religious leaders is thus firstly that they have no interest in, and no constructive help to offer for, the suffering poor of Pakistan. More than that, they are actually hangers-on of exactly the repressive powers of wealth that keep the people poor. Parwez explains that the *ulema* are corrupt in this way because they actually are not the guardians of true Islam. In

---

[1] Ghulam Ahmad Parwez, *Selim ke Nam*, vol. 1, Karachi, Idarah-i Tulu-i Islam, 1953, pp. 10-12.

his version of Islamic history, the whole structure of medieval law and theology was absolutely wrong. The reason was a belief in what he calls two kinds of revelation, recited and not-recited (*matlu* and *ghayr-i malu*).

He explains to Selim his version of how this mistake occurred. The Qur'an had fixed the punishment for adultery, but it had not fixed the punishment for drinking. Yet the Qur'an insisted that both crimes were evil. A non-Muslim might say that the omission means that the Qur'an is an incomplete book. Another answer is to say that whatever has not been fixed by the Qur'an has been fixed by the Prophet. According to this latter theory, there are two kinds of revelation.

Parwez claims that the belief in not-recited revelation is intended to establish a system in which an answer to every problem is given. The collections of Hadith were made by individuals a long time after the death of the Prophet. But Parwez is sure that the Prophet would never have left such an important part of religion to be looked after in such a haphazard way. Hadith, he insists, was not part of the religion as the people understood it.[2]

The course of this argument is intended to convince Selim that two kinds of religion have existed under the name of Islam. Parwez insists that in Pakistan two mutually exclusive systems are competing for allegiance—one based on the Qur'an alone, and the other based on Hadith.

His letters to Tahirah give further examples of his reasoning. As an imaginary representative of educated young Pakistani womanhood, she is assumed to find many of the teachings of the traditionalists distasteful. Parwez' answer is to assure her that such teachings are not the real and original Islam. For example, he comments that the usual Muslim belief in the superiority of man is based on the idea that the Qur'an teaches that man is the ruler (*hakim*) of woman. The verse in question is as follows:

"Men are in charge of women, because Allah hath made the one of them to excel the other."[3]

Parwez comments that the classical Muslim commentaries on the Qur'an such as that of Tabari were written in an age in which tyranny was common, and in which Christian, Jewish, and Magian (Zoroastrian) ideas on the low estate of women were influencing Muslim thought. He adds that false Hadith in which the inferiority of women was emphasized were prevalent. He says traditional Islamic thought concluded for these reasons that this verse meant the superiority of man. Parwez says that the true meaning of the verse is that man has the duty to provide sustenance. He insists that it in no way implies inferiority in women.

Tahirah is considered to be rebelling against the traditional Muslim ideas that in inheritance the woman's share should be half that of the man, and that the testimony of two women should be the equivalent of that of one man. Par-

[2] *Ibid.*, pp. 74-79.
[3] *Qur'an*, 4:34, trans. M. M. Pickthall.

wez says that from the Qur'anic point of view man is supposed to provide for the family, and woman is not supposed to bear this responsibility. This, he says, is the reason why man should inherit twice as much as the woman.

He adds, however, that if the man refuses his proper responsibilities then the estate should be divided according to the economic necessities of the situation. He emphasizes that woman, under what he believes to be the right system, should get less because her needs would be less, but he insists that this in no way means that she has fewer rights, or that she is a less valuable person than man.[4]

These examples indicate Parwez' method of attempting to reconcile apparently distasteful Qur'anic teaching with the values of a rebelling young contemporary. His primary insistence is that nothing Qur'anic could be distasteful, and therefore whatever is not liked must be the product of the false religion of the traditionalists. Many of the problems of Pakistan may have resulted from false religion, but the Qur'an itself is never to be held responsible for any ideas that have led to the oppression of human beings. Parwez' fundamental thesis is that the Qur'an is the authority which refutes the backward-looking traditionalists.

Parwez' rejection of the authority of the traditionalists is much more absolute than the criticisms of traditional authority made by Sayyid Ahmad Khan and Iqbal. The two earlier modernists had argued that the Shari'ah had been useful at an earlier phase of Muslim history, but that changed conditions of life made it necessary for the community to rethink what Sayyid Ahmad Khan had called the detailed application of the basic principles. Parwez, however, argues that the Shari'ah was always wrong since it was based on a wrong theory of revelation, and since it was articulated at a time when the Muslim community was governed by those whom Parwez considers corrupt, i.e., kings. Parwez is thus inviting his young readers to reject all of the Muslim past, with the exception of the lifetime of the Prophet and the first four Caliphs, as a period of darkness from which nothing can be learned.

The bleakness of Parwez' attitude to the Muslim past is echoed in his attitude to nature. In one respect, he follows Sayyid Ahmad Khan quite closely, namely in arguing that nothing miraculous is to be found in the Qur'an. He gives similar explanations of matters like angels, the crossing of the Red Sea, and so forth. He could be said to be arguing against supernaturalism in religion, and for natural explanations. But, on the other hand, he goes completely against Sayyid Ahmad Khan's belief in the natural capacity of man to know good.

In order to lead Selim to understand this lost condition of man, Parwez undertakes to disabuse him of the idea that 'natural man' is in any way in a good state. The seventeenth letter to Selim deals with the question of human nature. Parwez comments that it is generally believed that Islam is the religion of nature

⁴ Ghulam Ahmad Parwez, *Tahirah ke Nam*, Karachi, Idarah-'i Tulu-'i Islam, 1957, vol. 1, pp. 45-57.

(*fitrat*). It is also, he says, generally believed that human nature is made in accord with the nature of God (*'ayn Khuda ki fitrat*).

Parwez says that the phrase "Islam is the religion of nature" is so generally accepted among Muslims that few question it. He, however, refuses to bow down before the demands of blind acceptance of phrases without questioning their meaning. For centuries, he thinks, Muslims have talked of nature and human nature without understanding the meaning of the words. Parwez believes that the habitual use of meaningless phrases is related to the practice of blindly following customary beliefs and practices.

Parwez considers that the failure to think clearly is directly connected to the failure to act constructively. He recognizes that to implement a revolution, one must have clear and distinct ideas. He therefore wishes to discover the meaning of the phrase "human nature."

Parwez says that the definition of human nature is such a difficult matter that human thought has not been able to establish a clear answer to the problem. The East, he says, has followed blind *taqlid* (authority) in the matter, whereas the West has devoted much thought and research to an analysis of human personality.

Parwez outlines for Selim as follows what he believes to be the gist of Western thought on the problem of man. One school of thought believes in the existence of an essential human nature, not subject to the influence of heredity and environment. Parwez says that this cannot be right because of the evidence provided by the fact that children do not become human if left to grow up apart from people. A second school of thought believes that human characteristics have been gradually acquired through centuries of evolution. But, says Parwez, this cannot be true because certain common human characteristics have always been present.

He comments that a third school of thought is characteristic of the anthropologists. According to them, original human nature existed at the beginning of human history before the development of civilization. From this we must conclude that present-day aborigines are the most true manifestations of essential human nature. Parwez contends that this theory would make ignorance and the weaving of superstitious fantasies the ideal of human life.

The psychologists say that young children are closest to true human nature. Parwez urges Selim to study small children, and to observe their characteristics. They are self-centered and jealous. They are foolish; sometimes they put their hands in the fire. Parwez concludes that this theory also is unsound. Parwez thus rejects as unsatisfactory what he believes to be Western ideas as to the essential nature of man. He considers the belief that man can be understood and defined in terms of the characteristics of primitive men and children to be degrading.[5]

---

[5] Ghulam Ahmad Parwez, *Selim ke Nam*, vol. 1, pp. 283-287.

There seems to be in Parwez a strong feeling that man must have infinitely more potentialities than have yet been realized. Therefore he rejects what he considers to be the popular Muslim idea that man as he presently is manifests true human nature as formed by God. For the same reason, he rejects what he considers to be the Western idea that true humanity is seen in primitive men and children. Parwez seems to conclude that true human nature cannot be discovered by observing what man has so far been and done in history. He concludes that proper and fulfilled humanity can be manifested only after the example of 'true humanity' has been placed before men as a model.

In seeking such a model, he turns to the Qur'an. He comments that according to the story of Adam as narrated in the Qur'an, the angels complained to God that it was wrong for man, who was destructive, to be given authority. From this, Parwez concludes that the first basic attribute of man is destructiveness. Human history, he comments, confirms Qur'anic teaching in this matter. Other characteristics of mankind mentioned in the Qur'an are tyranny, ignorance, purposelessness, ungratefulness, preferring evil to good, and carelessness.

Parwez thus concludes that the Qur'an teaches that man in his natural state is ignorant, destructive, and tyrannical. Parwez sees this as confirmation of the observations he has made for man's behavior in the world, and in past history. Parwez holds that the Qur'an itself teaches the absurdity of the idea that man in his natural state is a true expression of human nature as God intends it to be.

He comments that the Qur'anic verse generally used as proof that Islam is a religion that approves and supports existing human nature is the following:

"So set thy purpose (O Muhammad) for religion as a man by nature upright—the nature (framed) of Allah, in which He hath created man. There is no altering (the laws of) Allah's creation. That is the right religion, but most men know not."[6]

Parwez contends that the Qur'an uses the word nature (*fitrat*) in a sense different from our contemporary understanding of the term. The Arabic of the Qur'an, he says, is the language of the Bedouin. He claims that only in later Muslim history were foreign philosophical ideas attributed to Qur'anic words. The original Qur'anic language was concerned with concrete things, not abstract concepts. He concludes that present-day Muslims have lost sight of the original meaning of the Qur'an because they have learned to think in terms of foreign concepts.

Parwez argues that *fitrat Allah* does not mean the nature of God. It means, he says, the laws of God's creation. The phrase "the nature of man" means that man is made according to the laws of God's creation. He contends that "laws of creation" means the system of nature. According to this system everything in the world develops according to its inherent potentialities. Similarly, man has latent potentialities in him. The purpose of life is to develop these potentialities. The only difference between man and the rest of the universe, according

---

[6] *Qur'an*, 30:30, trans. M. M. Pickthall.

to Parwez, is that man is free to choose whether or not to develop his potentialities.[7]

Parwez appears to believe that his Muslim contemporaries are complacent, inert and self-righteous because they believe that their natural state is somehow justifiable and acceptable in the sight of God. He thinks that they rationalize their sloth by believing that Islam is the religion of nature. In effect, he thinks that they have the notion that whatever is, is right.

His revolutionary zeal drives him to the opposite extreme, that of asserting that what presently exists is entirely wrong. Curses against Pharisees are a logical concomitant of a passion for change. A vivid image of the corruption of the present is a natural counterpart of almost any utopian vision. Parwez sees "natural man" as an undeveloped, animal-like creature, dominated by the instincts for self-preservation and the propagation of the species.

Parwez considers that the world as presently existing is the product of the activities of this destructive creature. He believes that "true" and "fulfilled" man would be something quite different, and that he would make an infinitely superior world. He believes that the Qur'an teaches man how to achieve this fulfillment and how to become "true man."

He says the Qur'an teaches that man is his natural, unguided state can only destroy himself. He also believes that the Qur'an puts before man the guidance that can lead him to the perfect fulfillment of all his potentialities. For Parwez, it is not possible for man by the use of his reason to arrive at any solution to the basic problems of life. He considers that reason is always the tool of emotion. He understands this to mean that "natural" man is always dominated by the animal drives for self-preservation and the propagation of the species. Reason, without the guidance of revelation, can do nothing more than help man to find means to fulfill his instinctive needs.

Parwez also contends that the natural man cannot have direct personal communication with God. By saying this, he is denying the validity not only of centuries of Muslim mysticism, but also of the prayers of all Muslims. He says that the one Qur'anic verse which might appear to contradict this—the well-known promise that God is as close to man as the vein in his throat—is unintelligible.[8]

Parwez' condemnation of mysticism is like his condemnation of the Shari'ah and the *ulema* in that his rejection is total. His thinking is that of a dualist for whom no shades of grey are possible. Mysticism is totally black for him because it has stood in the way of Muslims' achieving power and social justice in his lifetime. Sayyid Ahmad Khan and Iqbal had also condemned other-worldly and self-negating mysticism as an obstacle to Muslim action in the world. But neither of them said that individual religious experience as such was

---

[7] Ghulam Ahmad Parwez, *Selim ke Nam*, vol. 1, pp. 290-294.
[8] Ghulam Ahmad Parwez, *Man wa Yazdan*, Karachi, Idarah-'i Tulu-'i Islam, 1958, p. 396. *Qur'an*, 50:16.

inherently bad or impossible. On all these issues, Parwez is far more absolute in rejection of the past, and of traditional modes of religiousness, than his modernist predecessors.

The twentieth letter to Selim deals with the concept of God. As is usual in these letters, the author seeks first to discredit all the wrong ideas about God prevailing in the rest of the world and among present-day Muslims. He says that the flaw in all these wrong ideas is that they are subjective. God is understood differently by each person. Such subjective gods offer no reliable authority. He considers that all such subjective gods are products of the human mind, and that they have no relationship to the real objective God.

Parwez sees further proof of the absurdity of belief in a subjective God in the existence of situations in which different individuals in conflict with one another all pray to their own gods for help. Parwez asks for a God Whose authority shall apply equally to all men, and Whose existence shall be objectively true. Such, he believes, is the God Who speaks to man through the Qur'an.[9]

Parwez thus contends that man by his own efforts can in no way reach, or make contact with, God. If communication is to be established between God and men, the initiative must come from God.

Parwez upholds a strictly revelation-centered theory of life. Human intimations of immortality, in childhood or in any other phase of existence, are in no way valid for him. His mind seems to be dominated by rigidly systematic abstractions; he appears to require a simple, logical universe. He pays no heed to the subtleties and complexities of immediate existence. He takes it as an axiom that all human ideas, feelings, and intuitions about God are inherently false. Therefore the dimension of existence in which questions as to the divine quality of response to beauty or love arise is to him non-existent.

In Parwez' view, unguided man is totally lost. God, however, mercifully reveals guidance, and the lost is found. The saving initiative is entirely from God to man. Parwez believes that the purpose of revelation is to make known to man the attributes of God in order that man may perfect himself, discover his true being, by taking into himself these attributes. Parwez says the attributes form a model that should be the ultimate goal of every individual. He believes that the existence of this one goal for all men is the meaning of *tawhid* (unity).

Parwez contends that when human beings are totally committed to modelling themselves on the same pattern, it necessarily follows that harmony will develop among them. He considers that this is the only method by which human brotherhood can be established. Right actions follow necessarily from right faith. He insists that the proper development of individuals requires the proper structures of society. He believes that when all men are committed to modelling themselves on the same divinely revealed pattern, the ideal society

[9] Ghulam Ahmad Parwez, *Selim ke Nam*, vol. 1, pp. 350-357.

will necessarily come into existence. The fruit of this ideal society will be that all men will be devoted to the nourishing care of one another.[10]

One volume of Parwez' commentary on the Qur'an is devoted to the exposition of his view on the subject of the relationship between God and man. Parwez' method in this commentary is to collect from the Qur'an all the verses relating to a particular point, and to abstract from the collected verses a summary of the Qur'anic teaching.

He summarizes as follows what he considers to be the Qur'anic teaching as to the nature of God. God is the Life-giving, the Nourisher, the Sustainer, the Protector, the Giver of security and order, the Ever-watchful, the One in Whose grasp is profit and loss, the One Who knows the seen and the unseen, Ruler of all, the Master of glory, King of kings, the true Lord, the One Who is free from every defect, and the One upon Whom all depends.

Parwez claims that this is the objective God, the One Who speaks to man through the Prophets, the One Who could not be known by the unguided efforts of man. Parwez sees this God as a being Who can be known only through such revelation as He chooses to offer to man. He insists that no human efforts to reach the divine could ever lead to knowledge of the true God.

Parwez maintains that man cannot know the essence (*zat*) of God. Man can know nothing more than God's purpose for man as laid down in the Qur'an. According to Parwez, God plans the world according to his regular laws, as an engineer plans a machine. He says that *'amr* means God's original intention, and that *khalq* means his plan. He maintains that the physical universe is operated by God according to a clearly ordered plan.

For Parwez, the basic analogy that illuminates God's mode of operating, both in the physical universe and with man, is the seed and the tree. He believes that everywhere reality is the unfolding of potentialities that are latent and that are destined to develop according to a foreordained plan. The only difference that he recognizes in the case of man is that man is free to choose, or to reject, the proper mode of developing his potentialities.[11]

Parwez' choice of the work of the engineer as an analogy for the mode of operation of God is an illuminating instance of the general orientation of his mind. In other places in his writings, Parwez has used the term "machine" to describe both the system of the physical universe, and what he believes to be the right system for human life. It seems apparent that Parwez is concerned with the production of results. He admires the method that works, immediately and efficiently. For him, the great man is the builder of bridges, the changer of the face of the earth. He takes it as self-evident that the greatness of God must be seen in His power to effect change, and to improve the conditions of life in the world.

---

[10] *Ibid.*, pp. 358-361.

[11] Ghulam Ahmad Parwez, *Man wa Yazdan*, pp. 40-74. See also Ghulam Ahmad Parwez, *Islami mu'asharat*, Karachi, Idarah-'i Tulu-'i Islam, 1957, pp. 24, 25.

Parwez interprets the Qur'anic names or attributes of God in the light of this basic image of the engineer with the plan that will lead to paradise on earth. "God is merciful" means that God provides the plan that will permit man to develop fully his inherent potentialities. "God is independent" means that He depends on no one, and that He gives the help that all others need. "God sits on his throne" means that He is the center of the universe. "God is *mu'min* (faithful)" means that God gives security (the fruit of following the plan). "God is wise" means that He lays down the right principles for human life.[12]

Despite his rejection of the Muslim past, and the apparent "modernity" of Parwez' values, as indicated for example in his comments about women's rights, he does not hold up the West before Selim and Tahirah as a desirable model. On the contrary, he writes at considerable length to demonstrate that there has never been in any society, apart from the early Muslim community, a good way of life. The arrangement of material in his seven-volume commentary on the Qur'an gives some indication of the matters he thinks need discussing. The volumes are in Urdu.[13]

The volume entitled *What Has Man Thought?* is a survey of the whole of human history. The volumes *The Lightning of Sinai* and *The Veiled Flame* deal with Judaism and Christianity respectively. *Streams of Light* is concerned with prophets. *The Ascension of Humanity* is about Muhammad. *God and Man* and *Iblis [Satan] and Man* are the final two volumes.

Comparing the perspective of Parwez to that of the other two reformers is something like dealing with a half-truth or a caricature. He tries, as they did, to read widely and to come to grips with the thought of his age. He tries to put Muslim experience in the context of a view of world history as a whole. But the dualistic, or gnostic, quality of his mind leads him to see nothing in the human past but false religion, corrupt government and oppression. His touchstone is not the nature of Sayyid Ahmad Khan, but rather the perfect society he envisions. Measured by this yardstick, all that has been is bad, except for the one brief period when proper humanity was manifested.

The power of the devil in his view is expressed in the animal instincts to preserve the self and to propagate the species. Man cannot by his own efforts escape this power. Unless God intervenes directly, man will remain what he always has been, the victim of these demonic instincts. Parwez denies that either intuition or reason could lead man out of corruption. Supernatural intervention is necessary. By thus denying man's natural capacities, Parwez becomes much more dependent on the notion of intervention from outside than were his modernist predecessors. They had believed in the validity of reason and intuition. In this sense, Parwez is regressing to a form of supernaturalism, since for him nothing in man is trustworthy. He is also much more frightened and alone

[12] Ghulam Ahmad Parwez, *Man wa Yazdan*, pp. 53, 135-140, 278-286, 387, 403.
[13] For the Urdu titles, see *Ma'arifulu-l-Qur'an* in the bibliography.

in a hostile world. This alienation seems also to be characteristic of those he addresses.

What form shall the intervention take? Parwez believes that God has sent a plan for an ideal society. If men abide by that plan, their evil instincts will be overcome, and then justice and goodness will be possible. Once the plan is operating, human potentialities can be properly fulfilled.

The plan was in operation during the Prophet's lifetime, and that historical period is therefore the normative one for Parwez as it is both for the traditionalists and for the other modernists. Parwez does not take that period as literally normative in terms of modes of dress and social practice. Neither does he take his norm as the idea of a "world-transforming spirit" as the other modernists had done. Rather he takes the idea of a type of political system—namely, absolute obedience to a Divinely guided political center. In the first instance, that center was Muhammad. In the second instance, it was the rightly guided first four Caliphs. After that, corruption set in, and the Muslim community has lacked proper guidance for centuries. With the establishment of Pakistan, however, it ought to be possible to re-establish the proper system. Parwez uses the phrase "System of Divine Nurture" (*nizam-i rububiyat*) to describe the ideal he believes in.

The volume of Parwez' Qur'anic commentary that deals with prophets is entitled *Streams of Light*. Parwez sees each prophet as an archetype of a messenger from God to men. He considers that in each case the situation was the same: the prophet always brought a revolution-creating message, and he was always opposed by the forces of wealth, power, and priestcraft.[14]

This, as Parwez sees it, is the universal human situation. The implication would seem to be that contemporary Pakistan, and the contemporary world, stand before God in exactly the same manner as all other peoples have done. God intends the establishment of the system of divine nurture; the Qur'an proclaims this intention. The rich, the powerful, and the priests everywhere oppose this truth, and obscure and destroy the possibility of its proper implementation. Parwez concludes that the world is hell on earth because of man's failure to listen to divine guidance and to implement the system of divine nurture.

Parwez sees no real movement in history. For him, the conflict between the revolution-creating truth on the one hand, and the opposition of custom, priestcraft, capitalism, and political power on the other hand has everywhere and at every time been of the same order. He sees the stories of the prophets as given in the Qur'an as instances that point to factors that always exist in the archetypal human situation.

He finds one such instance in the story of Noah. He says that by the time of Noah divisions according to classes had come into being, as had domination

---

[14] Ghulam Ahmad Parwez, *Ju'e Nur*, Karachi, Idarah-'i Tulu-'i Islam, 1956, pp. 69, 70.

by priests. The story shows that the people of power, wealth, and religious authority always oppose the revolution-creating message because they realize that the prophet comes in order to snatch power from them, and to establish the system that will be in harmony with the laws of God. He says that the instance of Noah demonstrates that the oppressed classes respond to the revolutionary call. The Qur'anic verse in question says:

"They said: Shall we put faith in Thee, when the lowest (of the people) follow thee?"[15]

Parwez comments that in this case the people of wealth and power opposed the message, and that they therefore brought down on their heads the inevitable working out of God's law of retribution. Noah and the few who believed in his message were saved.[16]

Clearly, Parwez envisages contemporary Pakistan as another instance of this archetypal situation. The religious leaders of his time are thought by him to be of the same type as those who have always opposed prophets. His writings are intended to expose this situation, and thus to make possible implementation of the good society.

Parwez' writing is taken up much more with outlining the obstacles to the implementation of the system, than in exact description of how the ideal would work in practice. His purpose is to exhort Selim and Tahirah to throw off the false religion of the traditionalists, to get rid of capitalists and bad politicians, and to make way for the good system to appear. He argues that all the traditional practices such as prayer, fasting and pilgrimage have been wrongly understood. Only when the true system is implemented will these practices perform their proper role.[17]

He lists the following characteristics of the proper system:

1. Respect for man as man

2. The oneness of humanity

3. Human freedom

4. Co-operation

5. Justice

6. Restoring disturbed proportions

7. Consultation

8. An Islamic state as a common trust for the *ummat* (people) as a whole, and the justification for its existence as the doing of good for mankind at large.

[15] *Qur'an*, 26:111, trans. M. M. Pickthall.

[16] Ghulam Ahmad Parwez, *Ju'e Nur*, pp. 69, 70.

[17] Ghulam Ahmad Parwez, *Firdaws-i Gumgashtah*, Karachi, Idarah-'i Tulu-'i Islam, 1954, pp. 356-410.

9. Affairs of state entrusted to capable hands

10. Determination of nations on the basis of an ideology, as a Qur'anic permanent value.[18]

The main content of the permanent values as seen by Parwez seems to be obedience to the state with the understanding that the state will guarantee that the individual will develop fully; affairs of state are to be carried out in a spirit of co-operation and consultation, but all are to agree on the basic values. Parwez takes it as axiomatic that there exists an inherent human right to well-being.

"Every citizen has a right to be provided with work, basic necessities of life and means of development of his Personality."[19]

Commitment to this belief might be said to be one of the main motivating forces behind the writings of Parwez. His belief in the goodness of God seems to be intimately related to his conviction that the universe is so constituted that everyone has a right to well-being.

Parwez' delineation of the system of divine nurture seems to be an expression of his effort to say how this right to well-being can most rapidly be granted to everyone. He is convinced that a strong central authority will be necessary. He concludes that the Qur'an teaches that a strong central authority is necessary for the implementation of the system of divine nurture.

He claims that whenever the Qur'an says "God and the Prophet" it means "the central authority of the Islamic system of government." From this it follows that when the Qur'an admonishes men to obey God and the Prophet, it means obeying the central authority of the state.

"The agency for enforcing God's laws is the Islamic State and obedience to God means, in practice, obedience to the State which enforces His laws."[20]

Parwez thus seems to start with the conviction that everyone has a right to well-being, and to move from this belief to conclude that submission by all the citizens to the rule of the Islamic state is the only means by which this right can be granted. It is this aspect of his thought that particularly disturbs his Muslim critics.[21]

His belief in the necessity for a strong central authority would seem to be related to his idea that democracy has proved itself weak, and unable to act positively, constructively, and quickly. He writes at length about what he considers to be the failure of democracy.

"The latest political systems [sic] which human ingenuity has evolved is National Democracy, but it is also failing badly. Firstly, there are parties in the

---

[18] Ghulam Ahmad Parwez, *Islamic Ideology*, Lahore, Idarah-'i Tulu-'i Islam, n.d. [1957?], pp. 20-28.

[19] *Ibid.*, p. 23.

[20] *Ibid.*, p. 14.

[21] *Parwez ke bare men ulama ka mutafiqah faysalah ma'izafat-i jadidah*, Karachi, 1962.

system struggling constantly against one another, and secondly, there is rivalry and hatred among various countries and nations making the world a veritable hell."[22]

Democracy is rejected by Parwez because it gives sovereignty to the people, and because it recognizes finality in decisions arrived at by the vote of the majority. As we have seen, Parwez has a low opinion of natural man, and from this it follows that he believes that man cannot be trusted to make wise decisions, or to create a good world.

Parwez also believes that if the state does not live up to its God-given responsibilities, it should relinquish its power.

"But says God to the Islamic State—since you take obedience from the people in my name, you should give them what I have promised to give, that is, fulfil the responsibilities which I have assumed in respect of mankind. If you fail to fulfil the responsibilities to people, you lose your right to their obedience. The two go together. Therefore, in the Qur'anic Social Order, the relationship between the individual and the state is a two-sided affair: the individual obeys the laws of God through the agency of the State, and the State honours the promises God has made to man."[23]

Parwez does not appear to consider that matters might become difficult if the state controlled the armed forces, and if it did not choose to relinquish power. Yet there is certainly abundant evidence both in Islamic history and in Western history to demonstrate that this is the basic problem that arises when one tries to devise governing institutions. Parwez' failure to take this question seriously is perhaps an indication of his failure to take the lessons of history to heart.

In the system of divine nurture, there should be one strong central authority that should command the obedience of all the citizens. Parwez believes that this central authority should administer all the means of production of the community. He believes that much of the trouble in the world is the result of the fact that individuals have seized the means of production for themselves, have exploited others, and have left some people impoverished. As we have seen, he interprets every prophet's message from God as meaning that the means of sustenance should be taken out of the hands of individuals and handed over to the state, which would be set up in order to administer the means of sustenance in the interests of all believers. He writes as follows of his idea of the ideal economic system:

"Says the Qur'an:

"Allah has brought from the believers their lives and what they have of material things so that He may give them *Jannah*"—(9:111). [*Jannah* means paradise.]

"The meaning of the verse is that the people entrust their lives and property

[22] Ghulam Ahmad Parwez, *Quran's Political System*, Lahore, Idarah-'i Tulu-'i Islam, n.d., p. 17.

[23] Ghulam Ahmad Parwez, *Islamic Ideology*, pp. 14, 15.

to the State which undertakes to enforce the laws of God, and, in return, the State gives them *Jannah*. You know that there is a *Jannah* which is to come after a man's death, but the Holy Qur'an uses the term *Jannah* also for Social Order established here, on this earth, in which every individual is assured, and he is actually provided, all that is required for the development of his body and his personality, and is free from want, anxiety, and fear. According to the contract referred to above, therefore, the individual in affirming obedience to the laws of God surrenders, without any compensation, his life and property to the Islamic State, and in return the State assumes full responsibility for providing him the basic necessities of physical life and all the means required for the development of his Personality. By this arrangement, the individual, even after surrendering his life and property to the State, preserves his Individuality or Self, nay helps it develop and gain in strength day by day, and, on the other hand, the State gets established on firm and solid grounds. The laws of God through their observance by the individual as well as the State, ensure both the above objectives."[24]

It will be apparent that this view of the duties of the State is novel in Muslim thought. Parwez' opponents call it Communism, and he himself recognizes a need to distinguish between the Communist system and his idea of the system of divine nurture.

"But mind you, by this control over means of production the Islamic State does not become at par with a Communistic State. There is a world of difference between the two. A Communistic State, or for that matter of fact, any Secular State, has no inviolable principles to guide or control its activities. An Islamic State is, however, bound irrevocably by inviolable principles given by the Holy Qur'an."[25]

Parwez sees Communism as vague and wandering in the same sense as he conceives Western democracy to be directionless and lost. Both systems, in his view, fail to guarantee absolute security, because both fail to place before the individual and the state an objective, permanent pattern.

---

[24] *Ibid.*, pp. 15, 16.
[25] *Ibid.*, p. 17.

Conclusion

One indication of the attitudes of the traditionalists to the core of modernist ideas is a *fatwa* (opinion, ruling) which a number of Pakistani *ulema* issued against Parwez.[1]   Among the forty points listed as errors, there is a vigorous refutation of the idea that obedience to God and the Prophet should be interpreted to mean obedience to the State.   However, Parwez is also similarly condemned for accepting Darwin's theory of evolution, and for denying that Adam and Eve were historical personages.   The dilemma of the *ulema* seems to be pointed up by their inability to distinguish between the kinds of problems involved in these two issues.   The other points in the condemnation all exhibit a similar ability to recognize deviation from traditional ideas, along with inability to evaluate the possible validity of novel ideas.

The traditional modes of theological education have obviously trained men who can recognize that something is new, but who cannot undertake a critical analysis of either the appropriateness of their own convictions and practices to their situation, or of the possible truth of ideas coming from unexpected sources. This *fatwa* suggests that none of the innovative ideas of Sayyid Ahmad Khan or Iqbal have yet been critically assimilated by the *ulema* in question.   Since both the earlier reformers emphasized new methods of education as a fundamental key to the community's dilemmas, one can imagine that they would not be greatly surprised to know that theological education has not yet changed, and that the products of the theological schools are still neither ready nor able to attempt serious evaluation of modernist theories.   The greater pessimism of Parwez is evident here also, since he thinks the state must first be changed before education can be reformed.

Our original question as to how much authority the past should exercise is answered by all these modernists with the primary assertion that the Muslim community should continue and should prosper.   It isn't easy to know why any of us should affirm that we will continue the works begun by our ancestors. Muslims generally affirm this strongly, perhaps partly because they have so much to be proud of in their past, and also because their tradition imbues them with the conviction that they have never been subservient to others, and never should be.   They have no tradition of respect for Caesar.

This independent stance can be interpreted to mean no submission to non-

---

[1] *Parwez ke bare men ulama ka mutafiqah faysalah ma'izafat-i jadidah*, Karachi, 1962, pp. 34-38.

Muslim persons or systems. It can also mean, however, an insistence within the community on self-criticism in the light of transcendent standards of justice and mercy. The community is made up of persons whose ultimate allegiance is to God.

As long as the community is agreed that it should continue, and that the Qur'an is the source of guidance, the Muslims can hold together in spite of an increase in the diversification of opinion on theological questions. The authority of the Qur'an of course derives from God, but also, conversely, God is known because He has revealed Himself through the Book. The community's special identity derives from its relationship to God, as announced by the Qur'an.

The idea that the early Muslim period was a second foundation of normative importance after the Qur'an has been prevalent in the Islamic community for centuries. The modernists share this premise, although they differ from the traditionalists in their understanding of what constitutes the essence of the authority of that period. For the traditionalists, the matter has been thoroughly investigated and worked out as a result of the complex processes that went into the original gathering together and legitimating of the Hadith and the further process of working out the Shari'ah.

The modernist critique of Hadith and Shari'ah has based itself on new theories of what constitutes the true importance of the example of the first Muslims. Sayyid Ahmad Khan saw this essence in that the first Muslims were changed from a barbarous people into a civilized one. The good sense and practicality of the Prophet and his companions is thus the norm for him. Iqbal saw in this same period an example of creative dynamism. Parwez sees in it an instance of an all-powerful state.

One could say that each of these three is projecting onto the past his vision of a better future. However, it is also true that each gets his vision of the future in some degree from what he knows of the past. There is thus some truth in what each perceives about the past. The decision as to which aspect of a many-faceted historical period, such as that of the first four Caliphs, shall be normative remains critical. The direction of the leadership given the members of the community by Sayyid Ahmad Khan and Iqbal would be to help them resolve these dilemmas firstly by developing better ways of studying history so that the early community could be known as fully as possible, and secondly by developing institutions by which all Muslims, having been adequately educated both in knowledge of their past, and of contemporary problems, could evolve ways of deciding for themselves what appropriate responses to new situations might be.

Iqbal did not see absolute political authority as normative, because his reasoning always assumes that a future Muslim community will be one in which adequate education will prepare all the citizens to take part in a democratic manner. From this perspective, the absolute political authority of earlier periods of Muslim history, and the religious authority of an elite of religious scholars, were both temporary structures appropriate only for situations in which education was not general. One could imagine an argument between a follower of Iqbal and a follower of Parwez as to how much power the state should have. Both could attempt to justify their positions by appeal to the example of the first Caliphs. It is true that those Caliphs had a lot of power, and also that they consulted other people. The factors that might make a given Muslim see one or other facet of his model as the normative one are obviously complex. In part, these factors are related to confidence in reason, and to self-confidence in general. Both Sayyid Ahmad Khan and Iqbal exhibited confidence that no problems were so insurmountable that better educated and reasonable Muslims would not be able eventually to resolve them. Parwez is in striking contrast to his predecessors in his distrust of any instrument other than absolute political power as a means of change.

Islamic modernism has been characterized by an emphasis on the "this-worldly" aspect of God's guidance. Our three modernists are directing their attention to worldly problems such as how to change laws and to develop new educational and political institutions. They assume this concern to be a faithful response to God. They believe that the worldly success of the community has been evidence of God's favor, and that worldly failure implies some serious break in the community's relationship with God. The modernist challenge to the traditionalists is an accusation that the traditionalists are failing to understand what God requires under the changed circumstances of the community.

Such a perspective could lead men to think that any new thing that works, or produces results must be acceptable to God. Parwez comes close to such a position, and to its implication—that anything apparently unsuccessful, such as normal Muslim praying and fasting, must be offensive to God, or anti-God. The consensus of the community so far has certainly and understandably been against Parwez in respect to this latter issue.

Does the modernism of Sayyid Ahmad Khan and Iqbal contain any awareness that "difficult" judgments will have to be made about the rightness and wrongness of such new institutions and purposes as may develop, and any suggestion as to how such judgments should be made? Iqbal was perhaps more aware of this difficulty than his predecessor, although it is probable that they were not very far apart on these issues. The limits to what man can justifiably do lie in the realm of what is offensive to God. And the core of that is given in the Qur'an. These two considered that human reason could agree with the moral imperatives God had proclaimed in the Qur'an. In this matter also, these two reformers trusted that the community itself, as long as it was faithful to its origins, and as it improved its education, would be able to work out a reasonable consensus, and decide for the better and against the less good in matters of human behavior.

As we have indicated, Parwez is much more pessimistic about human reason than the other two. They tended to believe in change by evolution, whereas he explicitly calls for revolution. His demand is for immediate and total change of the conditions of life by which his fellow Muslims are entrapped. Patience has run out. His despair perhaps reflects also disappointment among some Pakistanis that the affirmative leadership of earlier reformers has not resulted in much improvement in the economic conditions of the people. His conviction that the communists are not much better than the capitalists when it comes to providing a really sound and healthy society is not unlike various other types of mid-twentieth century radicalism.

One cannot conclude a survey like this with much comment as to what might happen next, since the milieu in question is being subjected to so many stresses.[2] It is probable that the unselfconscious confidence that Sayyid Ahmad Khan had absorbed from his early years is becoming more rare with each succeeding generation. On the other hand, such a loss of certainty may be countered by educational methods that will produce Muslims who are conscious of their assumptions and their values, and therefore confident in a different manner. Iqbal himself is a kind of prototype of a man who gains his confidence from his knowledge. The question mark remains therefore in the area of how the tradition is to be transmitted.

One reason we cannot foresee the next phase of Pakistani thinking about religious questions is of course that we can hardly presume to predict what problems may be exercising the minds of the next generation. Holding the parts of the nation together is one pressing difficulty, and economic development naturally is creating many problems. Whether good relations with Western nations will increase or decrease is an open question, dependent on many factors, not least of which is the policies of those nations. Parwez is more bitterly anti-Western than Sayyid Ahmad Khan or Iqbal, and that fact may be a significant indication of the increased disillusionment of liberal Muslims with the West.

In suggesting that Iqbal might be a prototype, we had in mind the assumption that Muslims who had had an education equivalent to his might tend to think more or less as he did. If such an assumption has validity, then we need to ask whether his way of thinking has indeed been transmitted very effectively. With respect to the traditional modes of theological education in the *madrasas*, the answer seems to be that Iqbal's perspective has not yet been seriously studied. Whether it ever will be so studied remains a question. In the universities, there is at present no real emphasis equivalent to what is known in the West by such

---

[2] In the years following the establishment of Pakistan in 1948, conflict as to how much influence the traditional religious leaders should exercise has been more or less continuous. That has been one major problem for the new nation. Other major difficulties have been economic development, agricultural improvement, relations with India, and dispute as to the relative merits of democracy as opposed to army rule. Religious attitudes have necessarily been affected by all these matters. No comprehensive study has yet been done of all the diverse currents of religious thought and feeling that have been operative in Pakistan. On the specific issue of the tensions between the traditional religious leaders and the government, an excellent book is L. Binder, *Religion and Politics in Pakistan*, Los Angeles, University of California Press, 1961.

names as "religious studies." The Islamic Studies departments tend to avoid controversial areas. Philosophy departments are the principal places where students might be found studying Iqbal. Some students are thus working quietly away, but this kind of activity touches the main stream of the nation's life fairly little. Most of the activities in the universities are directed towards training students with skills for transforming the economic conditions of life— hence, technology is given a much higher priority than philosophy of religion.

And yet the young Selim and Tahirah have many troubles. Their feeling of identification is in part a question of whether they are proud of their own history, or whether, as in the case of Parwez, they think that their present difficulties are the results of the corruption of their predecessors. If they are proud of their past, do they envisage it as a "code for the whole of life," as the conservatives often say, or as an inspiration towards new and more nearly perfect manifestations of the values transmitted from the past? Among any group of Pakistani young people, adherents of all these positions would probably be found. It is not very cheering to contemplate the increase in bitterness that has taken place in the movement of thought and feeling from Sayyid Ahmad Khan and Iqbal to Parwez. But whether as students of Asian religions or as fellow citizens of the world, we need to keep an eye on each generation as it comes along. The rapidity of change is about the only assumption that can be taken as certain.

Bibliography

Abbot, Freeland, *Islam and Pakistan.* New York, Cornell University Press, 1968

Abid, Abdu-l-Karim, "Parwez sahib ke afkar ka shajarah-'i nasab," *Faran,* March, 1956

Ahmad, Aziz, *Islamic Modernism in India and Pakistan, 1857-1964.* London, Oxford University Press, 1967

Azad, Mawlana Abu-l-Karim, *The Tarjumanu-l-Qur'an,* ed. and trans. by Dr. Sayyid Abdu-l-Latif. London, Asia Publishing House, 1962

Arnold, Sir Thomas W., *The Preaching of Islam,* 2nd ed. London, 1913

Baljon, J. M. S., *Modern Muslim Koran Interpretation.* Leiden, Brill, 1961

————, *The Reforms and Religious Ideas of Sir Sayyid Ahmad Khan.* Leiden, Brill, 1949

Binder, Leonard, *Religion and Politics in Pakistan.* Los Angeles, University of California Press, 1963

Dar, B. A., *Religious Thought of Sayyid Ahmad Khan.* Lahore, Institute of Islamic Culture, 1957

Hali, Altaf Husayn, *Hayat-i Javid.* Lahore, Nur Company, reprinted 1957

Ikram, S. M., *Modern Muslim India and the Birth of Pakistan,* 2nd ed. Lahore, Sh. Muhammad Ashraf, 1965

Ikram, S. M., and P. Spear, eds., *The Cultural Heritage of Pakistan.* Karachi, Oxford University Press, 1955

Iqbal, Javid, ed., *Stray Reflections, a Notebook of Allama Iqbal.* Lahore, Sh. Ghulam Ali, 1961

Iqbal, Muhammad, *The Reconstruction of Religious Thought in Islam.* London, Oxford University Press, 1934; reprinted Lahore, Sh. Muhammad Ashraf, 1962

English Translations of Iqbal's Poetry:

    A. J. Arberry, trans., *Complaint and Answer.* Lahore, Sh. Muhammad Ashraf, reprinted 1961

    ————, *Javid-Nama.* London, Allen and Unwin, 1966

    ————, *The Mysteries of Selflessness.* London, John Murray, 1953

    ————, *Persian Psalms.* Lahore, Sh. Muhammad Ashraf, reprinted 1961

    B. A. Dar, trans., *Gulshan-i Raz-i Jadid and Bandagi Namah.* Lahore, Institute of Islamic Culture, 1964

    Tariq and Aziz, trans., *The Guide.* Lahore, Pan-Islamic Publications, 1965

    V. G. Kiernan, trans., *Poems from Iqbal.* London, John Murray, 1955

    R. A. Nicholson, trans., *The Secrets of the Self.* London, Macmillan, 1920

Khan, Sayyid Ahmad, *The Mohamedan Commentary on the Holy Bible.* Aligarh, 1863

————, *Tafsiru-l Qur'an* (6 vols.). Lahore, Matba'-i Gulzar-i Muhammadi, 1891

————, *Tahrir fi usul al-tafsir.* Lahore, Niwalkishor Steam Press, 1913. An unpublished English translation by D. M. Rahbar is in the library of the Institute of Islamic Studies, McGill University, Montreal.

————, *Tahzibu-l-Akhlaq* (2 vols.). Lahore, Malik Fazlu-d-Din, 1870-1876.

————, *Review on Dr. Hunter's Indian Musalmans Are They Bound in Conscience To Rebel Against the Queen.* Lahore, Premier Book House, n.d.

Kuchch Parwez ke bare men ulama ka mutafiqah faysalah ma'izafat-i jadidah. Karachi, 1962.

Letters of Iqbal to Jinnah. Lahore, Sh. Muhammad Ashraf, 1956.

Works by Ghulam Ahmad Parwez:
    Asbab-i zawal-i ummat. Karachi, Idarah-'i Tulu-'i Islam, 1952
    Badah-i zindagi. Karachi, Idarah-'i Tulu-'i Islam, 1956
    Fundamentals of Islamic Constitution. Karachi, Idarah-'i Tulu-'i Islam, 1956
    Iqbal awr Qur'an. Karachi, Idarah-'i Tulu-'i Islam, 1955
    Islami Mu'asharat. Karachi, Idarah-'i Tulu-'i Islam, 1954
    Islami Nizam. Karachi, Idarah-'i Tulu-'i Islam, 1952
    Islamic Ideology. Lahore, Idarah-'i Tulu-'i Islam, n.d. [1957?]
    Ita'at-i Rasul. Karachi, Idarah-'i Tulu-'i Islam, 1956
    Khum-i zindagi. Karachi, Idarah-'i Tulu-'i Islam, 1957
    Lughatu-l-Qur'an (4 vols.). Lahore, Idarah-'i Tulu-'i Islam, 1960, 1961
    Ma'arifulu-l-Qur'an (7 vols.). Karachi and Lahore, Idarah-'i Tulu-'i Islam.
        The volumes are entitled as follows:
        Barq-i Tur, 1956
        Iblis wa Adam, 1954
        Insan ne kiya socha?, 1955
        Ju'e Nur, 1956
        Man wa Yazdan, 1958
        Mi'raj-i Insaniyat, 1949
        Shu'lah-'i Mastur, 1958
    Mafhumu-l-Qur'an. Lahore, Idarah-'i Tulu-'i Islam, 1961
    Nizam-i Rububiyat. Karachi, Idarah-'i Tulu-'i Islam, 1954
    Quran's Political System. Lahore, Idarah-'i Tulu-'i Islam, n.d.
    Salim ke Nam (3 vols.). Karachi, Idarah-'i Tulu-'i Islam, 1957
    Tahirah ke Nam (2 vols.). Karachi, Idarah-'i Tulu-'i Islam, 1957
    Why do we lack Character? Lahore, Idarah-'i Tulu-'i Islam, n.d.
Rahman, Fazlur, *Islam.* London, Weidenfeld and Nicolson, 1966
Saiyidain, K. G. *Iqbal's Educational Philosophy,* 6th ed. Lahore, Sh. Muhammad Ashraf,
    [1965]
Schimmel, Annemarie, *Gabriel's Wing* (Studies in the History of Religions, Supplements
    to *Numen,* VI). Leiden, Brill, 1963
Spear, Percival, *A History of India,* Harmondsworth, Penguin Books, 1965
Vahid, Syed Abdul, *Iqbal, His Art and Thought.* London, John Murray, 1959
——————————, ed., *Thoughts and Reflections of Iqbal.* Lahore, Sh. Muhammad Ashraf,
    1964